Portfolio Management
for New Products

Portfolio Management for New Products

R.G. Cooper, S.J. Edgett and E. J. Kleinschmidt

Portfolio Study
McMaster University
Hamilton, Ontario

The publisher offers discounts on this book when ordered in quantity for special sales. For more information please contact:

Portfolio Study   or   Ph: 905-525-9140, ext. 27437
P.O. Box 194   Fax: 905-648-8331
McMaster University
1280 Main Street W
Hamilton, Ontario
Canada L8S 1C0

Canadian Cataloguing in Publication Data

Cooper, R. G., Edgett, S.J. and Kleinschmidt, E. J.

    Portfolio Management for New Products

    Includes bibliographical references.
    ISBN 0-920603-13-0

    1. Research, Industrial - Management. 2. Research,
    Industrial - Cost effectiveness. 3. Product management.
    4. New products. I. Edgett, Scott J. II. Kleinschmidt, Elko, J.
    III. Michael G. DeGroote School of Business. IV. Title

HD30.4.C66 1997   658.5'75   C97-930005-3

ISBN 0-920603-13-0

For further information please contact the authors directly at:

Michael G. DeGroote School of Business
McMaster University
1280 Main Street W
Hamilton, Ontario
Canada L8S 4M4
Ph: 905-525-9140

Robert G. Cooper   Scott J. Edgett   Elko J. Kleinschmidt
Ext. 23968   Ext. 27437   Ext. 23970
e-mail:
cooperr@mcmaster.ca   edgetts@mcmaster.ca   kleinsc@mcmaster.ca

Contents

Exhibits

Preface

A number of people and organizations have helped us in writing this book. The continued financial support of the research, that enabled us to write this book, was made possible partly from the Innovation Research Centre, Michael G. DeGroote School of Business, McMaster University and partly from Esso Chemical (Exxon Chemical Canada). Companies and people that provided us with insightful comments and their views on portfolio management included: Jens Arleth of U-3 Consultants, Denmark; Ed Bartkus of Rolm and Haas; Martin Brennan and Mike Harley of Reckitt & Colman; Bill Brennan of Esso Chemical, Canada; Tom Chorman of Procter & Gamble; Patricia Evans of Strategic Decisions Group; Bob Gill and Beebe Nelson of Product Development Partners, Inc.; Ray Kilminster of Hoechst U.S.; Wolf-Rüdiger Lange of Rhode & Schwarz; Dan Panfil of English China Clay; Alex Petit of New Product Consultancy, England; Kathryn Sachse and Marg Kneebone of the Royal Bank of Canada; and Dr. Gary Tritle of 3M.

Chapter 1

The Quest for the
Right Portfolio Management Process

Introduction

New products are vital to the success and future prosperity of the modern corporation. The period of downsizing which characterized the mid 80s to mid 90s is over: senior executives are beginning to sober up to the reality that no corporation ever shrank itself to greatness. As we move into the next millennium, the growth game is on – faster than ever. Front and center in this growth game is the desire for new products – successful, significant, winning new products. Driven by rapidly advancing technologies, globalization of markets, and increasing competition at home and abroad, effective new product development is emerging as *the major corporate strategic initiative* of the decades ahead. Those corporations which succeed at new product development will be the future Mercks, HPs, 3Ms and Microsofts; those companies which fail to excel at new products will invariably disappear or be gobbled up by the winners.

A vital question in this new product battleground is: How should the corporation most effectively invest its R&D and new product resources? That's what portfolio management is all about: resource allocation to achieve corporate new product objectives. Much like a stock market portfolio manager, those senior executives who manage to optimize their R&D investments – to define the right new product strategy for the firm, select the winning new product projects, and achieve the ideal balance of projects – will win in the long run. This book is about how winners manage their R&D and new product portfolio, and the lessons your company can put into practice in order to achieve a higher return from your R&D investment.

What Is Portfolio Management?

Portfolio management and the prioritization of new product projects is a critical management task. Roussel, Saad and Erikson in their widely-read book claim that "... portfolio analysis and planning will grow in the 1990s to become the powerful tool that business portfolio planning became in the 1970s and 1980s.".[25]

Portfolio management and project prioritization is about resource allocation in the firm. That is, which new product projects from the many opportunities the corporation faces shall it fund? And which ones shall receive top priority and be accelerated to market? It is also about corporate strategy, for today's new product projects decide tomorrow's product/market profile of the firm. Note that an estimated 50% of firms' sales today come from new products introduced within the last five years.[15,24] Finally, it is about balance: about the optimal investment mix between risk versus return, maintenance versus growth, and short term versus long term new product projects.

This book reports the results of an intensive study of portfolio management in industry. The purpose of this research was to investigate the current state of portfolio management; that is, how leading firms manage their new product portfolios and whether or not these approaches are really working. A second goal was to identify best practices and to make concrete recommendations about how firms should be going about managing their R&D (or new product development) portfolios.

The format of this book is as follows:

1. The remainder of this chapter provides background on the topic of portfolio management, helps shed light on why so many firms face difficulties in their attempts to allocate R&D resources, and defines the requirements for an *ideal* portfolio management approach. The chapter ends with some immediate conclusions from the study, and also a look at the three goals in portfolio management.
2. Next, we provide a close look at the methods that leading corporations employ to manage their new product project portfolios and to allocate their R&D resources. We also note the perceived strengths and weaknesses of each approach:
   - approaches used to maximize the value of the portfolio (Chapter 2);
   - approaches used to achieve a balanced portfolio (Chapter 3); and
   - approaches used to develop a strong link to strategy (Chapter 4).
3. Concluding observations are made regarding what appears to work in portfolio management, and what doesn't, and the pitfalls, hurdles and concerns management is addressing (Chapter 5).
4. Finally, we recommend ways in which portfolio management can be made more effective in your organization, and we propose some techniques and methods to make this happen (Chapters 6 & 7). Our recommended Portfolio Management Process is outlined in these final chapters.

What Happens When You Have No Portfolio Management

Companies without effective new product portfolio management and project selection face a slippery road downhill (see Exhibit 1.1). Indeed, many of the problems which beset product development initiatives in businesses can be directly traced to a lack of effective portfolio management.

First, no portfolio management means a strong *reluctance to kill* new product projects. There are no Go/Kill criteria and no consistent mechanism for evaluating and, if necessary, culling out weak projects. Projects seem to get a life of their own, running like express trains past review points. Further, new projects simply get added to the "active list" with little appreciation for their resource needs or impact on other projects. The result is a total *lack of focus*: far too many projects for the limited resources available.

The problems don't stop here. A lack of focus and too many active projects means that resources and people are *too thinly spread*. As a result, projects end up in a queue – serious log-jams in the process – and cycle time starts to increase. Suddenly there are complaints about projects taking *too long to get to market*. But worse: with resources and people thinly spread, everyone starts to scramble – too many balls in the air. And the result is predictable: *quality of work starts to suffer*. For example, the essential up-front homework isn't done, and needed market studies designed to build in the voice of the customer are left out due to lack of time and people. Poor quality execution of these and other tasks, steps and stages in the new product process means *an increase in failure rates.*[7] So, not only are projects late to market, their success rates drop!

There's more: No portfolio management means no rigorous and tough decision points, which leads to poor decisions. The result is *too many mediocre projects* in the pipeline: too many extensions, minor modifications and defensive products, which yield marginal value to the company. And so, many of the launches yield disappointing and "ho hum" results: there is a noticeable *lack of stellar new product winners*. Even more insidious, the few really *good projects are starved* for resources, so that they're either late to market, or never achieve their full potential. And that creates a huge opportunity cost which never appears on the P&L statement!

The problems don't end there. Without a rigorous portfolio method, the *wrong projects* often get selected, and for all the wrong reasons. Instead of decisions based on facts and objective criteria, decisions are based on politics, opinioneering, and emotion. Too many of these ill-selected projects simply fail!

Exhibit 1.1: What Happens When You Have No Portfolio Management Method

No portfolio management means...	Immediate Result	End Result: Poor New Product Performance
A reluctance to kill projects Many projects added to the list A total lack of focus	Too many projects - people & resources thinly spread Projects in a queue Quality of execution suffers	Increased time to market Higher failure rates
Weak Decision Points Poor Go/Kill decisions	Too many mediocre, low value projects: - tweaks & modifications Good projects are starved	Too few stellar product winners Many "ho hum" launches
No rigorous selection criteria Projects selected on emotion, politics	Wrong Projects are selected	Many failures
No strategic criteria for project selection	Projects lack strategic direction Projects not strategically aligned	Scatter gun effort New products do not support business strategy

The final negative result is strategic: Without a portfolio management method, strategic criteria for project selection are missing, and so there is *no strategic direction* to the projects selected. After all, new products are the leading edge of business strategy: They define tomorrow's vision of your company! But without a portfolio method, projects are *not strategically aligned* with the business's strategy; and many strategically unimportant projects find themselves in the pipeline. The end result is a *scatter gun effort* which does not support the business's strategic direction.

The price for not having an effective portfolio management and project selection method for new products is very high. If your business faces any of these problems – a lack of stellar new products, long cycle times, a high failure rate, and lack of strategic alignment – perhaps the root causes can be traced back to ineffective portfolio management. So read on, and find out what others are doing about the challenge, and most importantly, what your company can do!

Three Decades of R&D Portfolio Methods: What Progress?

The challenge of portfolio management in product development is not new. Over the decades, the topic has surfaced under various guises including "R&D project selection", "R&D resource allocation", "project prioritization" and "portfolio management". By the early 70s, dozens of articles had appeared on the topic, with most authors only making one stab at the topic before moving on to more fruitful fields. The majority of these early proposed methods were *management science, optimization techniques*. To the management scientist, this portfolio management problem was one of constrained optimization under conditions of uncertainty: a multi-project, multi-stage decision model solved by mathematical programming. Thus, the original portfolio selection models were highly mathematical, and employed techniques such as linear, dynamic and integer programming. The objective was to develop a portfolio of new and existing projects to maximize some objective function (for example, the expected profits), subject to a set of resource constraints.

Anyone familiar with these programming techniques will immediately recognize the hurdles that the mathematician and management scientist would have solving this portfolio problem. Further, in spite of the many methods proposed in the early days, there was a remarkable lack of follow-up: for example, few authors ever described attempts to actually implement their methods and to gauge their feasibility; indeed, the articles appear to be largely the result of academics writing to and for each other. In spite of the importance of the topic, no guru or "dominant school of thought" ever emerged here, perhaps an indication of the frustrations faced in seeking solutions.[1,2,3,12,20]

More recent years have witnessed a number of other proposed new product portfolio methods. These include, for example:

- ▸ Financial models and financial indices, ranging from traditional NPV, IRR and payback methods through to various financial ratios (such as the Productivity Index).[4,22]
- ▸ Scoring models and checklists, where projects are rated and scored on a

variety of qualitative questions (in some cases, the project score becomes the criterion for project prioritization).[16,25,32]

- ▶ Probabilistic financial models, including Monte Carlo Simulation and decision trees.[27]
- ▶ Behavioral approaches, designed to bring managers to a consensus (or to individual decisions), such as Delphi, Q-Sort and analytic hierarchical modelling (paired comparisons).[21,27,33]
- ▶ Mapping approaches, essentially extensions of the original SBU portfolio models (the BCG model: stars, cash cows, dogs, wildcats; or the GE/McKinsey model), where various parameters are plotted against each other in a bubble diagram format – plots such as Reward versus Probability of Success.[22,25]

In spite of all the proposed solutions, a recent benchmarking study points to *project selection* and *project prioritization* as the weakest facet of all new product management activities.[9,10] Management in the 161 business units studied confessed to a lack of project prioritization, too many projects for the available resources, and minimal attempts at portfolio management. So there is a major gulf between theory and practice: While the published literature over the past 30 years outlines many approaches for portfolio management and project selection, there is very little evidence regarding the actual transfer of these techniques into management practice. It is not surprising to find that companies continue to flounder here. Thus the question remains: How do and should companies select the appropriate portfolio of new product investments?

Portfolio Management: It's Not So Easy

Why then has the goal of an effective portfolio management process been so elusive? Before charging into the topic of what techniques work best, let's stand back and reflect on what portfolio management is, and why portfolio management has been such a difficult challenge to management.

We define portfolio management as follows:

> Portfolio management is a dynamic decision process, whereby a business's list of active new product (and R&D) projects is constantly up-dated and revised. In this process, new projects are evaluated, selected and prioritized; existing projects may be accelerated, killed or de-prioritized; and resources are allocated and re-allocated to the active projects. The portfolio decision process is characterized by uncertain and changing information, dynamic opportunities, multiple goals and strategic considerations, interdependence among projects, and multiple decision-makers and locations. The portfolio decision process encompasses or overlaps a number of decision-making processes within the business, including periodic reviews of the total portfolio of all projects (looking at all projects holistically, and against each other), making Go/Kill decisions on individual projects on an on-going basis, and developing a new product strategy for the business, complete with strategic resource allocation decisions.

New product portfolio management sounds like a fairly straightforward exercise of decision-making and resource allocation. But there are many unique facets of the problem which make it perhaps the most challenging decision-making task faced by the modern business:

- First, unlike traditional portfolio models (e.g., the BCG or GE/McKinsey models), R&D portfolio management focuses on *what might be* - new opportunities, new products, new ventures. Note that traditional portfolio models focus on *what is*, namely existing SBUs. Because new product portfolio management deals with future events and opportunities, much of the information required to make project selection decisions is at best uncertain, and at worst very unreliable. But still the decisions must be made!

- Second, the decision environment is a very *dynamic* one. The status and prospects for projects in the portfolio are ever changing, as results of new studies become known, market or technical tests are completed, and new competitive and market information emerges. What looked like an excellent project just six months ago now suddenly is not so promising. Additionally, new opportunities are constantly being discovered – opportunities which vie for resources and compete with existing projects.

- Next, projects in the portfolio are at *different stages* of completion. Some are at the early stages, where little is known about the project. Others are approaching commercialization and launch, where forecasts and data are somewhat more reliable. The dilemma is that all projects compete against each other for resources, so that comparisons must be made between projects at different stages, each with different amounts and "goodness" of information.

- The problem is made more complex by recognizing that *resources* to be allocated across projects are *limited*. That is, a decision to fund one project may mean that resources must be taken away from another. Additionally, projects are not totally independent of each other: for example, the talents needed to work on one project may also be vital for another; conversely, undertaking one project may actually facilitate another – there exist synergies between projects. Finally, resources are not infinitely flexible: unlike money, people cannot always be immediately transferred in a seamless fashion between projects.

- The final facet of portfolio management which makes the decision process so difficult is that portfolio management is critically important. At one time, new product project selection and allocation of R&D resources was thought to be "an R&D thing", and left largely in the hands of the technical community. Not so today, as senior management recognizes that new products are the leading edge of business strategy, and so new product choices are virtually synonymous with strategic choices.

Requirements for an Effective Portfolio Management Process

Given the lackluster performance of many existing portfolio management approaches coupled with the reluctance of industry to adopt most of the methods, there is no shortage of prescriptions about what the ideal portfolio management method should be and do. Reflect for a moment on some of these requirements, especially as we review the many portfolio methods in use in industry in the next three chapters.

1. *Corporate goals, objectives and strategies must be the basis for new product (or R&D) portfolio selection.*[12,13,14,16,18,19,27,29,30]

More than ever, the management of technology and R&D is viewed as *strongly linked to corporate strategy* and the firm's competitive success.[12] This is especially true for multinational corporations, which face a much broader scope of possible strategic directions: portfolio management must be congruent with the overall strategy of the business;[14] indeed it is the embodiment of that strategy! Portfolios in many Japanese firms, for example, tend to stress continual technological improvement (a long term strategy) aimed at constant product improvement (incrementalism, a major aspect of the R&D effort), and have resulted in positive performance.[11] Your portfolio analysis and resource allocation must be intimately linked to strategy formulation.[32]

2. *Senior management is the driver of strategy and hence must be closely involved in new product (or R&D) project selection decisions.*[5, 8, 11,12,16,18,19,32]

This is a parallel theme. Traditionally, senior management has been involved in R&D to the extent that they periodically review research programs, projects and staff to assess progress and to determine the contribution that each makes to the corporate goal.[4] Today, however, there is a *need to go beyond this*, given that technology and strategy are inseparable.[7] Thus, the organizational context in which R&D project selection and resource allocation occurs must be considered when one develops appropriate project selection methods.[19] This means that the cooperation and active involvement of top management, who direct the long term strategy, is essential if R&D efforts are to be properly focused.[19]

3. *Better communication and understanding must exist between senior corporate management and R&D management.*[12,27,28]

One problem with the adoption of some of the more sophisticated and quantitative portfolio models is the gulf between R&D management and senior corporate management. Senior executives often lack a strong research background, while R&D people lack the skills to communicate in an understandable and credible fashion with senior executives. This communication impasse mandates a portfolio selection method which not only effectively selects projects, but also manages R&D programs and projects *and their communication* to top management.[12] Senior people must have consensus on key issues (e.g., new product goals or project priorities) – something which is often lacking – and ensure that this common position is understood lower down in the firm.[28]

4. *Portfolio methods must mesh with the decision framework of the business.*[4,14,16,19,27,29]

The organizational context in which new product or R&D project selection and resource allocation occurs is a fundamental consideration in the development of appropriate decision methods.[19] For example, there is growing recognition that project selection tools should be used to ask questions of the entire organization. "Picking the right projects" is a meaningless exercise unless the whole organization is involved and emotionally committed to the final set of selected projects.[27] For large multinational corporations, the problem is more complex. Here portfolio decisions must be made seeking buy-in from multiple business units, across geographic boundaries, and at the corporate level.[14] One way to involve senior management in the decision process is by integrating selection models into interactive decision support systems.[19]

5. *Portfolio methods should be used for information display only, and not yield an optimization decision.*[4,5,13,16,29]

This conclusion almost flies in the face of logic. In the early days, the assumption was that management wanted the model to yield a decision recommendation: for example, *a prioritized list of the right projects*. The fact is that managers are less interested in the final result of the method than in the *process* itself. The value for them is in systematically stepping through each project and assessing its status as a project and how it fits with the corporate strategy and objectives.[4,5] For example, the provision of a risk/reward (or risk/return) map or matrix, often obtained via highly subjective methods, does not yield an optimum solution (e.g., no list of best projects) or even an analytical tool to arrive at such a solution. But it is recommended as an effective tool and guideline for managers – a visual representation of the entire set of possible projects – for use throughout the whole process of portfolio selection.[13] Yet another recommended approach is *fuzzy modelling*, whose flexibility permits switching from maximizing behavior to *satisficing behavior* with respect to some or all goals.[29] This method permits the manager to investigate, in an interactive fashion, different scenarios in response to different new product aspirations.

6. *The selection method employed must accommodate change and the interaction of goals and players.*[13,26,29,30]

Portfolio methods must be able to deal simultaneously with resource interaction, benefit interaction, and outcome interaction among and between projects. To date, *no model has been proposed* which can do all three.[26] Further, the system must be flexible. It must adapt to the reality that goals, requirements and project characteristics change during the life-time of projects.[13] For example, if the manager modifies his/her aspirations, the system must adjust and compute a new compromise solution.[29] Finally the system must enable managers to plan how the active project list evolves over time: which new projects are added to the list, when, and what role each should play in the total portfolio.[30]

7. *The portfolio selection method must accommodate decision-making at different levels in the organization.*[6,19,30]

Project selection decisions are made at different levels in major corporations. Some projects conducted within business units are independent or stand-alone efforts; others, such as platform programs or cross-BU projects, involve several business units or divisions, and so sub-projects within each business unit are highly interdependent. Clearly, the selection approach used must be able to handle both types.[6] The choice of levels in the problem hierarchy for R&D project selection must consider the organization structure and the nature of the decision-making process for these various types of projects.[19]

8. Risk must be accommodated by the selection technique.[17, 23,28,31]

One facet of strategy is deciding on the acceptable risk level within a chosen portfolio, and finding ways to minimize (or manage) risk.[28,31] Therefore, risk, uncertainties and probabilities of success must be somehow built into the portfolio model and be visible in the project selection process.[23] Another way of handling risk is via diversity; and so diversity or portfolio balance must also be a consideration.

Where We Stand

In spite of the challenges outlined above, progress has been made!

- Classical schemes, such as *scoring and sorting models,* have been modified and adapted to become more relevant as portfolio selection aids. While useful for ranking projects on financial, strategic and other criteria, however, they often fail to capture concerns about the *right balance of projects in the portfolio.*

- New *mapping approaches* and bubble diagrams have gained adherents because they greatly simplify the portfolio problem, and they provide a visual representation of the choices faced. Mapping is perhaps too new to assess its impact, but there are already some problems: mapping projects on a two dimensional matrix may be a little too simplistic (after all, portfolio management is a complex problem, difficult to boil down to a few maps and a handful of dimensions); the maps that focus on financial rewards have been criticized for being too financially driven; while maps that consider numerous strategic and other qualitative factors yield far too many maps for the executive to digest.

- *Mathematical programming* portfolio and project selection models have become more realistic in recent years.[1] Such models are now able to integrate multiple constraints, multiple time periods, differing goals and objectives, and other parameters into a single choice model.

- Finally, there is the recognition that no one model gives the *right answer.* Instead, hybrid approaches are being developed that permit a more tailored approach to portfolio selection.

---

[*]   See for example 4,6,16,19,26,29.

New product portfolio selection has become a central management issue. The business climate of today requires faster decisions, better allocation of scarce resources, and clear focus. Given that corporate revenue streams are heavily dependent on successful new products, and that technology strategy is intimately linked to corporate strategy, *effective portfolio management is more than ever central to corporate prosperity.*

With no clear answers available from the literature, and strong evidence to suggest that management has rejected many of the proposed approaches, a number of provocative questions still remain. For example, what is the current state of portfolio management in industry today? How do senior managers handle the portfolio question inside their own organizations? How are they linking strategic direction to R&D decisions? Are the approaches that companies use producing the desired results? And what are the strengths and weaknesses of these approaches?

Portfolio Management Practices in Leading Firms

How are various firms handling portfolio management? The next three chapters tackle this topic, and begin a portrayal of portfolio methods used by a selection of companies that are known to be actively using or developing and implementing a portfolio management approach. Before we delve into the details of these models, let's first consider some of the important research results which became evident immediately: that is, conclusions regarding project selection and some of the problems these companies faced (or had faced) when it came to new product project selection and portfolio management.

- **A critical problem:** Every company we interviewed believed the portfolio management, project selection and resource allocation problem to be critical to new product success. Virtually all companies had experienced considerable problems regarding project selection. And with resources tighter than ever, the issue of proper resource allocation and picking the right projects was paramount. Further, the desire to see the business's strategy reflected in its portfolio of R&D investments was another driver of improved portfolio management techniques. As a result, many of the firms contacted were devoting a considerable amount of effort to solving the portfolio problem.

Some of the specific problems faced by companies in project selection and portfolio management, which were creating the sense of urgency, are familiar ones:

- **Does not reflect strategy:** Many businesses or SBUs had enunciated business strategies. In some cases, they even had developed new product strategies for the business – strategies which defined the goals for new products (e.g., by year five, 32% of sales revenue will be generated by products we do not now have); the role that product development would play in achieving overall business goals (e.g., 60% of our SBU's growth will come from new products; another 30% from market developments; and 10% from market size increases); and even strategic arenas of focus – what product types, markets and technologies (or platforms) would generate these new products. The problem lies in linking these strategies – business and new product – to spending on R&D projects. A breakdown of R&D spending by project types often revealed serious disconnects between goals/strategies of the business and where the money was spent.

- **Poor quality portfolios:** Executives were generally displeased with, or at best doubtful about, their firms' current portfolio of projects. Many new product projects were thought to be weak or mediocre ones; others were considered unfit for commercialization; and success rates in the marketplace were less than adequate. As one executive put it: "We implemented our portfolio management approach [a risk/reward bubble diagram model], and the first thing which became evident was that half our projects were in the wrong quadrants, including some of our big ones! By the end of the year, the list of projects had been cut in half." Similar audits had resulted in similar cuts in other firms, leading one to doubt the quality of current portfolios.

- **Tunnels, not funnels:** Another related problem is that Go/Kill decision points – the gates in new product processes – were often perceived to be ineffective. In too many companies, projects tended to get a life of their own, and little could stop them once they gained momentum. In one leading firm, an internal audit of 60 current projects

---

How the Research Was Undertaken

Interviews were conducted in 35 leading firms in various industries. Some companies were singled out for in-depth interviews, on the basis of the uniqueness and proficiency of their portfolio approach. (For example, two companies had an on-going task force in place for more than a year to "solve" the portfolio management problem; another company we interviewed in-depth had spent more than $500,000 on external consultants to arrive at their "portfolio solution").

The companies, although quite willing to share the details of the portfolio approaches with us, were promised that we would not reveal any details of any project under development – all illustrations use disguised projects. Some of these leading firms included:

- A major multinational chemical company (Hoechst-U.S.) - in the top three in the world.
- A major industrial materials supplier (English China Clay) - the number one in its industry in the world.
- A major high technology materials company.
- A major financial institution (in the top five in North America).
- A multinational consumer goods company.

Three of the five were in the US. Additionally, another 30 companies provided data on their portfolio methods, experiences and outcomes. Note that the method of sample selection was purposeful (not random). We were deliberately selecting firms according to their experience, proficiency and ability to provide insights regarding portfolio management. During the in-depth interviews, the details of the portfolio approaches used, the rationale, problems faced and issues raised were all investigated.

---

revealed that 88% resembled an express train "... slowing down at stations [projects reviews], but never with the intention of being stopped!" Only 12% were handled in a thoughtful way with rigorous Go/Kill decision points. Even when killed, the complaint in some firms was that projects had a habit of being resurrected, perhaps under a new name.

We observed that criteria for making Go/Kill decisions were inadequate or not used, and often a mechanism for rating, prioritizing or even killing projects was lacking. As one frustrated manager exclaimed: "We talk about having a funnelling process which weeds out poor projects; heck, we don't have a funnel, we have a tunnel ... ten concepts enter the process, ten go into Development, ten go to Launch ... and one succeeds!"

- **Scarce resources, a lack of focus:** Resources are too scarce to waste on the wrong projects. Indeed, a common complaint was that product development was suffering from too lean resources, especially in areas such as marketing and manufacturing/operations people. Most firms confessed to having far too many projects for the limited resources available. The result was that resources were spread very thinly across new product projects, so that even the best projects were starved for people, time and money. The end result was that projects were taking too long to reach the market. Many key activities – such as upfront homework, getting sharp, early product definition, and building in the voice of the customer – were not being executed as well or consistently as they should have been. The bottom line was that there was *a lack of focus*, which created a plethora of other problems.

- **Trivialization of product development:** A final problem brought on by a lack of resources (or a lack of focus) was the trivialization of product development in some firms. The quest for cycle time reduction together with the desire for more new products than ever, when coupled with the resource constraint, led many firms to do the obvious: pick "low hanging fruit" – projects that could be done quickly, easily and cheaply. Often these projects were trivial ones – modifications, extensions – while the significant products, which were the ones needed to yield real competitive advantage and major breakthroughs, were often placed on the back-burner. The net result was a portfolio of projects which was very short-term, while projects designed to create tomorrow's winners or technology platforms for growth were missing.

No Quick Answers

No company we interviewed had totally resolved the portfolio management problem. In spite of all that has been written, there are *no magic answers* here. More over there is not even a "preferred" or dominant method. The quest for the ideal portfolio management and project prioritization and selection method continues!

Many of the techniques presented in this book are quite new to the companies involved. For example, a major consumer goods company and a materials firm had both set up task forces to deal with the problem one year before our interviews, and even at the time of the interviews, were only in the early stages of implementation. We saw much the same in other firms as well – new, relatively untried methodologies being implemented. Thus the reader should treat some of the techniques described as "exploratory" and "experimental" rather than "tried-and-proven" methods.

Three Goals in Portfolio Management

While the portfolio methods employed in firms varied greatly, the common
nator across firms was the goals management was trying to achieve. One or more of
three high level or macro goals dominated the thinking of each firm we studied,
either implicitly or explicitly. The goal most emphasized by the firm seemed to influence the choice of portfolio method. These three broad or macro goals were:

- **Maximization of Value:** To some firms, the preoccupation was to allocate resources so as to maximize the value of the portfolio in terms of some company
  objective (such as long term profitability; or return-on-investment; likelihood of
  success; or some other strategic objectives). These *maximization of value* methods are outlined in Chapter 2.

- **Balance:** Here the principal concern was to develop a balanced portfolio – to
  achieve a desired balance of projects in terms of a number of parameters. For
  example, the right balance in terms of:
  - long term projects versus short, fast ones;
  - high risk, long shots versus lower risk, sure bets;
  - the various markets the company is in (one doesn't want all one's new prod-
    uct resources targeted at only one market);
  - different technologies or technology types (e.g., embryonic, pacing, base);
    and
  - different project types: new products, improvements, cost reductions, f u n -
    damental research.

  Portfolio methods aimed at securing *the right balance* of projects are the topic of
  Chapter 3.

- **Strategic Direction:** The main focus here was to ensure that, regardless of all
  other considerations, the final portfolio of projects was strategically aligned and
  truly reflected the business's strategy – that the breakdown of spending across
  projects, areas, markets, etc., was directly tied to the business strategy (e.g., to
  areas of strategic focus that management had previously delineated); and that all
  projects were "on strategy". Chapter 4 highlights these *strategically oriented* portfolio methods.

What becomes clear is the potential for conflict between these three high level goals.
For example, the portfolio which yields the greatest NPV or IRR may not be a very
balanced one (it may contain a majority of short-term, low risk projects; or is overly
focused on one market). Similarly, a portfolio that is primarily strategic in nature
may sacrifice other goals (such as likelihood of success). What also became clear in
our interviews was that although executives did not explicitly state that one of the
goals above took precedence over the other two, the nature of the portfolio management tool elected by that firm certainly indicated a hierarchy of goals. This was
because certain of the portfolio approaches uncovered were much more applicable to
some goals than others. For example, the visual models (such as maps or bubble
diagrams) were most amenable to achieving a balance of projects (visual charts being an excellent way of demonstrating balance); whereas scoring models tended to

be very poor for achieving or even showing balance, but most effective if the goals were maximization of value against an objective. Thus the choice of the "right" portfolio method depended on which goal management had explicitly or implicitly focused on.

Some Definitions

Before we move into the results of our study of leading firms' current practices, first, here are some definitions of terms we use throughout the rest of the book:

Stage-Gate Process: This is the formal process, or road map, that firms use to drive a new product project from idea to new product launch. This process typically has multiple stages, together with gates or decision points. A Stage-Gate process has many variants; it is also called *the new product process*, *gating process*, or *phase-review process*. Such a process is important to portfolio management, because the gates are where Go/Kill decisions are made on individual projects, and hence where resources are allocated. If your company has such a Stage-Gate process, then it must be included as an integral facet of the total portfolio approach.

Portfolio Review: This is the periodic review of the portfolio of all projects. It may take place once or twice annually, or even quarterly. Here, all projects – active projects and even those on hold – are reviewed and compared against each other. This Portfolio Review often uses portfolio models (defined below) to display lists or maps of the current portfolio. The vital question in the portfolio review is: Do we have the right combination of active projects here? Is this really where we want to spend our money?

Portfolio Models: These are the specific models or tools used to select projects and/or review the portfolio. They include scoring models, bubble diagrams and maps, various charts, financial models and strategic approaches. These are outlined in Chapters 2 to 4.

Portfolio Management Process (PMP): This is the *entire method* for project selection and portfolio management. It includes all of the components defined above.

Business Unit (BU): This is the smallest unit in the company for which portfolio management is undertaken. Usually a BU (or SBU) is a semi-autonomous, self contained business with its own goals, strategy and resources. For example, a BU likely has its own R&D budget. For smaller firms, the BU may be the entire company.

Business Strategy: This is the strategy for the BU. It specifies the goals, direction and areas of focus for the BU.

New Product Strategy: This is a component of (or flows from) the BU's business strategy. It specifies the BU's new product goals, direction and areas of focus (i.e., areas where the BU will focus its product development efforts). It may even specify desired levels of R&D and new product spending in specific arenas of focus (e.g., how much to spend in certain markets or product categories).

So read on and witness the details of the portfolio approaches that we found to be the most effective in achieving the three goals of portfolio management.

Chapter 2

Portfolio Management Methods: Maximizing the Value of the Portfolio

Goal #1: Maximizing the Value of the Portfolio

The first goal of most firms we studied was to maximize the value of the portfolio of projects against one or more business objectives (such as profitability, strategic, risk, etc.). A variety of methods were used to achieve this goal, ranging from financial methods through to scoring models. Each has its strengths and weaknesses. The end result of each method is a rank ordered list of projects, with the projects at the top of the list scoring highest in terms of achieving the desired objective(s): the value of the portfolio in terms of that objective is maximized.

Expected Commercial Value (ECV)

The ECV method seeks to maximize the value or *commercial worth* of the portfolio, subject to certain budget constraints. This approach is one of the more well-thought-out financial models. It features several new twists which make it particularly appropriate to portfolio management. We found it in use at a major US producer of clay and materials, English China Clay:

> ECC International (English China Clay) is the world's largest producer of clay and clay-related products, with annual sales revenues of about $4 billion (US). US operations are headquartered in Atlanta, Georgia. Clay products are sold into a myriad of different markets and applications, including fine paper (clay is what makes paper white and bright), and extenders and fillers for plastics, paints, and other materials. Even though clay is a rather mature business, ECC's aggressive management has an objective of a 30% increase in revenue derived from new products over the next five years.

In this ECV method, English China Clay determines the value or commercial worth of each project to the corporation, namely its Expected Commercial Value. This approach is based on a decision tree shown in Exhibit 2.1; it considers the future stream of earnings from the project, the probabilities of both commercial success and technical success, along with both commercialization costs and development costs. ECC's version of the ECV scheme also incorporates the *strategic importance of the project*, a feature the company added to the general ECV model in Exhibit 2.1.

Exhibit 2.1:   Determination of Expected Commercial Value of Project
(ECC uses a slightly modified version of this)

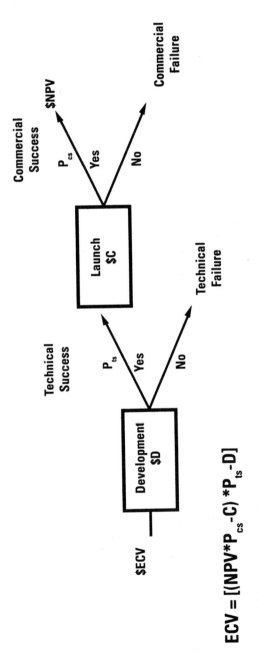

$$ECV = [(NPV*P_{cs} -C) *P_{ts} -D]$$

ECV = Expected Commercial Value of the Project

P_{ts} = Probability of Technical Success

P_{cs} = Probability of Commercial Success

D = Development Costs remaining in the project

C = Commercialization (Launch) Costs

NPV = Net Present Value of project's future earnings (discounted to today)

Based on a decision tree analysis (see Exhibit 2.1), the formula for the ECV is:

$$ECV = (NPV*SI * P_{CS} - C) * P_{TS} - D$$

where:

NPV	=	Net Present Value of ten year cash flow, after launch (none of the project costs – development, capital, etc. – have been subtracted from this stream; this NPV is strictly the income stream).
SI	=	Strategic Importance Index. This has three levels, depending on the strategic importance of the project (High, Medium, Low = 3,2,1).
P_{CS}	=	Probability of Commercial Success (from 0.20 to 1.00, in increments of 0.20 based on established criteria).
C	=	Commercialization (Launch) costs (capital costs, customer trials, marketing costs).
P_{TS}	=	Probability of Technical Success (again 0.20 to 1.00, in increments of 0.20, based on established criteria).
D	=	Development Costs (remaining in the project).

A sample calculation is given in Exhibit 2.2, with disguised projects from the company. Note how different the ECV is from the NPV; thus, merely rating or ranking projects according to NPV could be very misleading.

Exhibit 2.2: ECC's Determination of Expected Commercial Value

Project Name	NPV	Probability of Technical Success	Probability of Commercial Success	Development Cost*	Commercialization Cost*	ECV
Alpha	30	.80	.50	3	5	5.0
Beta	63.75	.50	.80	5	2	19.5
Gamma	8.62	.75	.75	2	1	2.1
Delta	3	1.00	1.00	1	0.5	1.5
Echo	50	.60	.75	5	3	15.7
Foxtrot	66.25	.50	.80	10	2	15.5

* Development cost (or Commercialization cost) remaining in project.

In order to arrive at a prioritized list, ECC considers scarce resources: in their case, capital resources are thought to be the constraining or scarce resource (note that many of ECC's projects are very capital intensive; for example, requiring new plant equipment). Other companies may chose to use R&D people or work-months, or R&D funds, as the constraining resource: most firms have a finite annual R&D budget and finite number of people. In the illustration borrowed but disguised from ECC, we've used R&D dollars as the constraint, and have set a budget of $15 million as a dummy figure to illustrate*.

---

* Note that ECC uses exactly the same routine to maximize the portfolio's value, except with capital as the constraint.

ECC then takes the ratio of what it is trying to maximize - namely the ECV - divided by the constraining resource, namely the annual R&D spending proposed per project. Projects are rank ordered according to this ratio, thereby ensuring the greatest "bang for buck"; that is, the ECV is maximized, for a given R&D budget*. Exhibit 2.3 shows the final prioritized list, with a horizontal line noting the point where the budget of $15 million is exceeded. Projects above the line are considered "active and in the portfolio"; those below the line are placed on hold. Note that had ECC's projects simply been rank-ordered according to the ECV alone (rather than the ECV/R&D ratio), the prioritized list would have been quite different. And most important, the resulting list would have yielded a lower total ECV value for a given R&D budget!

Exhibit 2.3: ECC's Ranked Ordered List According to ECV/Dev
(Note: Total Development Budget of $15 Million)

Project Name	ECV	Development Cost (Dev)	ECV/Dev	Sum of Dev
Beta	19.5	5	3.90	5.0
Echo	15.7	5	3.14	10.0
Alpha	5.0	3	1.67	13.0
Foxtrot	15.5	10	1.55	(23.0)
Delta	1.5	1	1.50	14
Gamma	2.1	2	1.05	15

Criterion: ratio of what you are trying to maximize divided by constraining resource (yields maximum "bang for buck").

This ECV model has a number of attractive features. Because this formula is based on a decision tree approach, it recognizes that if the project is halted partway through, certain expenses are not incurred, and that the Go/Kill decision process is a step-wise or incremental one. (For example, the simplistic route adopted by some – namely multiplying the NPV of a project by its probability of success – fails to capture this subtlety. The latter method distorts the value of projects, and in particular, unfairly over-penalizes projects with high capital or commercialization costs, and low probability of technical success.) A second feature is that all dollar amounts are discounted to today (not just to launch date), thereby appropriately penalizing projects that are years away from launch. A third benefit is that sunk costs – money already spent on

---

*   This decision rule of "rank order according to the ratio of what one is trying to maximize divided by the constraining resource" seems to be an effective one. We did simulations with a number of random sets of projects (much like the disguised list in Exhibit 2.2), and found that this decision rule worked very well - truly giving "maximum bang for buck"!

R&D or Commercialization – are not considered. Another feature is that the model, although largely financially based, does consider the strategic importance of projects. Finally, the model recognizes the issue of constrained resources and attempts to maximize in light of this constraint: the notion of "maximum bang for buck" rather than just "maximum bang".

A careful review of the equation in Exhibit 2.1 and the rank-ordering model in Exhibit 2.3 reveals that certain types of projects will be appropriately favored by this ECV model. Projects which this model will prioritize more highly:

- ▸ are those closer to launch (distant projects are penalized);
- ▸ have relatively little left to be spent on them – all money spent so far is a sunk cost, hence is not relevant to the ranking decision;
- ▸ have higher likelihoods of success (commercial and technical probabilities), and a higher stream of earnings; and,
- ▸ utilize less of the scarce or constraining resource (in ECC's case, projects with smaller R&D annual costs and lower capital requirements*).

The major weakness of the method is the dependancy on financial and other quantitative data. For example, accurate data on all projects' future streams of earnings, on their commercialization (and capital) expenditures, on their development costs, and on probabilities of success must be available. Often these estimates are unreliable, leading to doubts about the validity of the ranking method; or at best, these estimates are simply not available early in the life of a project, hence the method can only be used for projects past a certain point in the process (e.g., after a full financial business case has been developed). For example, one seasoned executive took great exception to multiplying two very uncertain probability figures together: "This will alway unfairly punish the more venturesome projects!". A second weakness is that the method does not look at the balance of the portfolio – at whether the portfolio has the right balance between high and low risk projects, or across markets and technologies. A third weakness is that the method considers only a single criterion – the ECV – for maximization (although admittedly, this ECV is comprised of a number of parameters).

If ...

- ▸ your company is very financially-oriented;
- ▸ good financial data and profitability estimates are available fairly early in the life of a project (i.e., profitability and commercial assumptions are typically fairly predicable);
- ▸ and there is a major constraining resource (so that maximization of bang for buck is the goal),

then the ECV method has many merits. We recommend that you at least consider it over other, more simplistic financial methods.

---

* But this could be any constraining resource, such as people (FTEs). The same type of calculations would apply.

Productivity Index

The *productivity index (PI)* is similar to the ECV method described above, and shares many of its strengths and weaknesses: the PI also tries to maximize the financial value of the portfolio for a given resource constraint. We saw the method in use in two firms - one, a medical products firm in the US; the other, a nuclear firm in the UK. The method has been popularized by Strategic Decision Group.[3]

The Productivity Index is:

$$PI = [ECV * P_{ts} - R\&D] / R\&D$$

Here, *expected commercial value (ECV)* is a probability-weighted stream of cash flows from the project, discounted to the present, and assuming technical success*. P_{ts} is the probability of technical success, while *R&D* is the R&D expenditure remaining in the project (note that R&D monies already spent on the project are sunk costs and hence are not relevant to the decision). Projects are rank ordered according to this index in order to arrive at the preferred portfolio.

Dynamic Rank Ordered List

The next method overcomes the limitation of relying on only a single criterion to rank projects witnessed above. We've labelled it the Dynamic Rank Ordered List approach, although Company G** simply called it their "portfolio model". This method has the advantage that it can rank order according to several criteria concurrently, without becoming as complex and as time-consuming as the use of a full-fledged, multiple-criteria scoring model. These criteria can include, for example, profitability and return measures; strategic importance; ease and speed to do; and other desirable characteristics of a high priority project. Exhibit 2.4 provides an illustration using disguised projects and data from Company G. The four principle criteria used by this company are:

- ► *The NPV* (net present value) of the future earnings of projects, less all expenditures remaining to be spent on the project. This NPV value was considered an important objective by Company G, in that it captured both the fact that the project exceeded the acceptable hurdle rate, and also denoted the sheer magnitude or impact of the project on the company – the "bang". Note that this NPV has built into it probabilities of commercial success (in the calculation of the NPV, sales revenues, margins, etc. have all been multiplied by probabilities to account for uncertainties).

- ► *The IRR* (internal rate of return) is calculated using the same data as the NPV, but gives the percent return. This was an equally important criterion for Company G, as it captures the efficient utilization of capital – namely "bang for buck".

---

*   Note that the definition of *expected commercial value* here is different than that used by English China Clay (Exhibit 2.1).

**   Some companies preferred not to have their names mentioned.

▶ *The Strategic Importance* of the project – how important and how aligned the project is with the business's strategy – is a key criterion to rank projects at Company G. Importance was gaged on a 1-5 scale, where 5 = critically important.

▶ *The Probability of Technical Success* was also an important consideration in ranking projects for Company G, as some projects were very speculative technically.

How are projects prioritized or ranked on four criteria simultaneously? Simple: First, the probability of technical success is multiplied by each of the IRR and NPV to yield an adjusted IRR and NPV– (see Exhibit 2.5). Next projects are ranked according to each of the three criteria: IRR adjusted; NPV adjusted; and strategic importance. Exhibit 2.5 shows this procedure, with the numbers in parentheses showing the rank orders in each of the three columns. The overall rankings – the far right column in Exhibit 2.5 – are determined by calculating the *mean of the three rankings*. For example, in Exhibit 2.5, for Project Alpha, which scored first on Strategic Importance, and second on each of IRR and NPV, the mean of these three rankings is 1.67, which places Alpha at the top of the list. Simple perhaps, but consider the disguised list of projects in Exhibit 2.5, and try to come up with a better ranking yourself – one that maximizes all three criteria!

The major strength of this dynamic list is its sheer simplicity: Rank order your projects on each of several criteria, and take the means of the rankings! Another strength is that the scheme can handle several criteria concurrently without becoming overly complex. Its major weakness is that the model does not consider constrained resources (as did the ECV model above, although conceivably Company G could build this into its rank ordering scheme), and like the ECV and PI models, it is largely based on uncertain, often unreliable financial data. Finally it fails to consider the appropriate balance of projects.

Exhibit 2.4: Company G – Dynamic Rank Order List
Six Projects & Data for Prioritization

Project Name	IRR* (%)	NPV ($ millions)	Strategic Importance**	Probability of Technical Success
Alpha	20%	10.0	5	80%
Beta	15%	2.0	2	70%
Gamma	10%	5.0	3	90%
Delta	17%	12.0	2	65%
Epsilon	12%	20.0	4	90%
Omega	22%	6.0	1	85%

* The hurdle rate is 10% IRR.
** Strategic Importance scale is a 1-5 rating, where 5=critically important.

Exhibit 2.5: The Six Projects Rank Ordered

Project Name	IRR'PTS	NPV'PTS	Strategic Importance**	Ranking Score*
Alpha	16.0 (2)	8.0 (2)	5 (1)	1.67 (1)
Epsilon	10.8 (4)	18.0 (1)	4 (2)	2.33 (2)
Delta	11.1 (3)	7.8 (3)	2 (4)	3.33 (3)
Omega	18.7 (1)	5.1 (4)	1 (6)	3.67 (4)
Gamma	9.0 (6)	4.5 (5)	3 (3)	4.67 (5)
Beta	10.5 (5)	1.4 (6)	2 (4)	5.00 (6)

* The final column is the mean across the three rankings. This is the score that the six projects are finally ranked on. Project Alpha is number 1 while Project Beta is last.

Note:
- Both IRR and NPV are multiplied by Probability of Technical Success.
- Projects are then ranked according to the three criteria. Numbers in parentheses show the ranking in each column. Projects are ranked ordered until no more resources.

Scoring Models

Scoring models have long been used for making Go/Kill decisions at gates; they also have applicability for project prioritization and portfolio management. Here, a list of criteria are developed to rate projects – criteria that are thought to discriminate between high priority and low priority projects. Projects are then rated by evaluators on each criterion, typically on 1-5 or 0-10 scales with anchor phrases. Next, these scores are multiplied by weightings, and summed across all criteria, to yield a Project Score for each project.

Although many firms we interviewed professed to be using such scoring models, either they were poorly crafted models (for example, inappropriate criteria), or there were serious problems in the actual use of the model at management decision meetings. Hence such models often fell into disuse. The key seemed to be in the construction of an appropriate list of scoring criteria – ones which really do separate winners from losers – and a method to gather the data and use the model at a management meeting.

Hoechst-US Corporate Research & Technology (HCRT) had constructed one of the best scoring models we've seen: it took several years of refinement, but the eventual model is so well-conceived that we report it here.

Hoechst AG is one of the largest chemical companies in the world, with annual sales in excess of $30 billion US. The particular unit studied was the Corporate Research & Technology in the US (HCRT), a research and technology intensive unit within the corporation whose special mandate is to develop and commercialize new products which lie outside the scope of the traditional business units. It tends to focus on larger, higher risk, more step-out and longer term major projects (as opposed to projects designed to maintain and renew a business unit's existing product line). Hoechst-US spends approximately $300 million on R&D, of which a significant portion goes to HCRT. It also uses a Stage-Gate new product process – a five stage-and-gate process designed to move projects from the idea stage through to commercialization.

The scoring portfolio model comprises a list of 19 questions within five major categories. Each question or criterion had been carefully selected and worded, operationally defined, and tested for validity and reliability over some years. We offer their model in Exhibit 2.6 as an example to other companies.

The five major factors which Hoechst considers in prioritizing projects are:

- ▶ Probability of technical success.
- ▶ Probability of commercial success.
- ▶ Reward (to the company).
- ▶ Business strategy fit (fit with the business unit's strategy).
- ▶ Strategic leverage (ability of the project to leverage company resources and skills).

Within each of these five factors are a number of specific characteristics or measures (19 in total), which are scored on 1-10 scales by management. The 19 scales are anchored (scale points 1, 4, 7 and 10 are defined) to facilitate discussion (see Exhibit 2.6 for the questions and their operational definitions).

Simple addition of the items within each factor yields the five factor scores. Then the five factor scores are added together in a weighted fashion to yield an overall score for the project, namely the *Program Attractiveness* score. This final score is used for two purposes:

1. *Go/Kill decisions at gates:* Embedded within Hoechst's new product process are pre-defined decisions points or gates. These gates are staffed by a group of senior managers and executives, who review the projects under consideration, and make Go/Kill decisions. The *Program Attractiveness Score* is one input into the Go/Kill decision at each gate: a score of 50% of maximum is the cut-off or hurdle. Note that the decision is not quite as simple as a "Yea/Nay" based on this score. There are animated discussions at the gate, where opinion and experience of managers surfaces, and where other issues and qualitative factors not captured in the 19 measures are dealt with. These gate meetings take place about once per month and are facilitated by an outside "referee", who walks the gatekeepers through the scoring model, and computes and records the scores.

2. *Prioritization:* Immediately following the gate meeting, the portfolio of projects is reviewed. This is where the prioritization of "Go" projects from the gate takes place, and where resources are allocated to the approved projects which were positively rated at the gate meeting. Here, the *Program Attractiveness* scores for the new projects (versus scores for already resourced projects) determines how the new projects are prioritized in the total list, and whether or not these new ones

Exhibit 2.6: Hoechst-US – Scoring Model

Factor 1: Probability of Technical Success

Program Title: _____   Date: _____

Key Factors	Rating Scale				Rating	Comments
	1	4	7	10		
Technical "Gap"	Large gulf between current practice and objective; must invent new science	"Order of magnitude" change proposed	Step change short of "order of magnitude"	Incremental improvement; more engineering in focus		
Program Complexity	Difficult to define; many hurdles	Easy to define; many hurdles	A challenge; but "do-able"	Straight-forward		
Technology Skill Base	Technology new to the company; (almost) no skills	Some R&D experience but probably insufficient	Selectively practiced in company	Widely practiced in company		
Availability of People and Facilities	No appropriate people/facilities; must hire/build	Acknowledged shortage in key areas	Resources are available; but in demand; must plan in advance	People/facilities immediately available		

Continued....

Factor 2: Probability of Commercial Success

Key Factors	Rating Scale				Rating	Comments
	1	**4**	**7**	**10**		
Market Need	Extensive market development required: no apparent need	Need must be highlighted for customers; product tailoring required	Clear relationship between product and need; one-for-one substitution of competitor's product	Product immediately responsive to customer need; direct substitute for existing company product		
Market Maturity	Declining	Mature/Embryonic	Modest growth	Rapid growth		
Competitive Intensity	High	Moderate/High	Moderate/Low	Low		
Commercial Applications Development Skills	Must develop; new to company	Must develop beyond current limited use	Need to tailor to proposed program	Already in place		
Commercial Assumptions	Low probability/ low impact	Low predictability/ low impact	High probability/ high impact	High predictability/ high impact		
Regulatory/ Social Political Impact	Negative	Neutral	Somewhat favorable (e.g. waste minimization, reduce hazardous materials in process)	Positive impact on high profile issues (e.g. plastics recycle)		

Continued....

Factor 3: Reward

Key Factors	Rating Scale				Rating	Comments
	1	4	7	10		
Absolute Contribution to Profitability (5 year cumulative cash flow from commercial start-up)	<$10MM	$50MM	$150MM	>$250MM		
Technology Payback	>10 years	7 years	5 years	<3 years		
Time to Commercial Start-up	>7 years	5 years	3 years	<1 year		

Factor 4: Business Strategy Fit

Key Factors	Rating Scale				Rating	Comments
	1	4	7	10		
Congruence	Only peripheral fit with business strategies	Modest fit, but not with a key element of the strategy	Good fit with a key element of strategy	Strong fit with several key elements of strategy		
Impact	Minimal impact, no noticeable harm if program dropped	Moderate competitive, financial impact	Significant impact, difficult to recover if program unsuccessful or dropped	Business unit future depends on this program		

Continued....

Factor 5: Strategic Leverage

Key Factors	Rating Scale				Rating	Comments
	1	4	7	10		
Proprietary Position	Easily copied	Protected but not a deterrent	Solidly protected with trade secrets, patents; serves captive customer	Position protected (upstream and downstream) through a combination of patents trade secrets, raw material access, etc.		
Platform for Growth	Dead end/ One-of-a-kind	Other opportunities for business extension	Potential for diversification	Opens up new technical and commercial fields		
Durability (Technical and Market)	No distinctive advantage; quickly "leapfrogged"	May get a few good years	Moderate life cycle (4-6 years) but little opportunity for incremental improvement	Long life cycle with opportunity for incremental improvement		
Synergy with Other Operations within Corporation	Limited to single business unit	With work, could be applied to another SBU	Could be adopted or have application among several SBUs	Could be applied widely across the company		

Continued....

Program Attractiveness Score: Summary of Scores on Five Factors

Abbreviated Form

Key Factors	Rating Scale				Rating	Comments
	1	4	7	10		
Probability of Technical Success	<20% probability	40% probability	70% probability	>90% probability		
Probability of Commercial Success	<25% probability	50% probability	75% probability	>90% probability		
Reward	small/breakeven	Payback >7 years	Payback = 5 years	Payback < 3 years		
Business Strategy Fit	R & D program is independent of business strategy; also low SBU impact	Somewhat supports SBU strategy; moderate impact	Supports SBU strategy; moderate impact	Strongly supports SBU strategies; high impact		
Strategic Leverage	"One-of-a-kind"/ dead end	Several opportunities for business extensions	Opportunities to transfer to another SBU	Vast array of proprietary opportunities High impact		

receive resources or are placed on hold. Other considerations, besides the computed *Attractiveness* score, are:

- ▸ appropriate balance or mix of projects;
- ▸ resource needs of each project (people, money); and,
- ▸ availability of key people and money.

Obtaining the Data

The method of data collection for input to the portfolio model is relatively straightforward for the first three techniques outlined in this chapter, namely the ECV, Productivity Index and the Dynamic Rank Ordered List. All use largely financial data to rank projects. These financial data are usually presented at the Go/Kill or gate meeting as part of the project's business case. Moreover, there are most often only a few key criteria, such as NPV, ECV or IRR, to be considered.

By contrast, scoring models use many more criteria (witness the 19 criteria used by Hoechst), and most of these are subjective in nature. This means the decision-makers themselves must "provide" much of the data (in the form of ratings based on subjective opinion) right at the review meeting. As a result, one of the recurring and frequently mentioned problems with scoring models is the actual use of the model at a gate meeting. The model can become cumbersome: Requiring decision-makers to rate and score projects at a meeting is time-consuming (and something many senior people are loathe to do), and collecting this data in a time-efficient manner during the meeting is difficult.

Several companies have solved some of this "data collection" problem by passing out a scorecard to the evaluators during the meeting. Here, a facilitator walks the decision-makers through the criteria one at a time. After some discussion, the facilitator calls for each evaluator to score the project on that criterion (privately and independently), and then moves to the next criterion. The scorecards are collected after all criteria are evaluated, and quickly tallied on an overhead transparency for display and discussion. Consensus and/or alignment are reached, and a decision on the project made. While not the neatest meeting format, this scorecard procedure does seem to work.

One major North American financial institution, the Royal Bank of Canada, also relies heavily on a scoring model – a much simpler one than Hoechst – but the *scoring methodology* is sufficiently unique that it merits mention here.

> The Royal Bank of Canada (RBC) is the largest bank in Canada, and one of the largest financial institutions in North America. It is a multi-branch bank with branches around the world, 50,000 employees, and assets of $120 billion (US$). Although much of its business is retail (i.e., to consumers), its *Business Banking division* is where significant advances have been made in new product and portfolio management.

The method involves the use of both a *sorting technique* and a *scoring model*. All the *new* and *existing* projects from the various product lines (Product Groups*) in RBC are considered – together and against each other - since they all compete for the same resource pie.

The portfolio analysis is a critical all-day meeting, to which the Product Group heads and other knowledgeable managers are invited. RBC is a heavy user of technology in their meeting rooms, and the portfolio meeting is no exception. An electronic meeting room is used, where every attendee has a computer and keyboard in front of him or her; when issues arise, attendees can type in text, which then appears on the computer screens of others in the room. The facilitator can also call for votes on issues. For example, "Now that we've discussed the revenue potential of this project, I'd like you to vote on this, scoring it from 1 to 9, where ....". Attendees then key in their scores; the results are tallied and displayed on each attendee's computer screen, including various statistics (means and deviations) or rank ordered lists; some discussion takes place; and then the meeting moves to the next issue or vote.

This electronic scheme has proven very effective in soliciting and integrating views from a diverse group of people in the room (everyone gets a chance to be heard) and also for gaining closure on each issue in a time efficient manner (via the electronic vote). Note that these are quite senior people, yet even they have adapted to the new meeting technology.

In RBC's process, almost 200 projects competing for the same pool of resources are under consideration. Almost half of these are relatively small, *non-discretionary* projects – vital maintenance work, minor systems changes and up-grades, and necessity work – and are automatically "in the budget". The remaining budget must then be allocated across *discretionary* projects, both *new* and *existing* product development projects. Prior to the portfolio meeting, each Product Group meets informally to discuss its own list of priorities.

The main portfolio meeting begins with a brief description of each of the roughly 100 discretionary projects (attendees have received a listing of these and some description prior to the meeting). Voting begins via a *sorting technique*: the facilitator requests each attendee to select his/her top 15 projects and their bottom 15 (all votes are keyed in via attendees' computers). The results of this *sorting vote* are displayed on the screens. The usual pattern is this:

- ▶ A subset of the more obvious projects, including many which are well-underway, receive quite a few positive votes each – there is general concurrence on these.
- ▶ Similarly, a subset receive a number of negative votes each – these are the obvious "kill" projects.
- ▶ A group of projects are in the middle – few votes and/or mixed positive and negative votes. These are flagged for discussion.

---

*   Product Groups in Business Banking include: Loans; Deposits; EDI; Payroll; Trade Products; Cash Management; and a host of other products/services provided by RBC to its corporate clients.

At this point, any attendee is allowed to *lobby* for any project in the *middle group*. Note that the very positive and very negative projects are not discussed as there was general concurrence on these. Only the uncertain ones (the exceptions) are debated.

Next, the facilitator calls for a *scoring vote* (1-9 ratings) for each project on each of four criteria:

- ▶ Does the project increase revenue?
- ▶ Does it reduce costs?
- ▶ Does it improve the quality of the bank's financial portfolio?
- ▶ Does it improve customer satisfaction?

Rating scores, averaged across evaluators, are added for each project to yield a *Project Score* (maximum score: 36), which is then converted to a percent – see Exhibit 2.7 for an example. (At one time, RBC applied weights to these criteria; however, the choice of weights caused much debate; thus more recent scoring sessions have simply assigned *equal weights* to all four criteria.)

Following this sorting and scoring session, a prioritized list of projects is generated and rank ordered *according to the Project Scores.* In this respect, the model so far is somewhat similar to the scoring approach used by Hoechst. Also shown on the list is the *expected annual expenditure* for this project, as well as the *cumulative spend* (the sum of all spending for all projects on the list, above and including this project) – see sample using disguised projects in Exhibit 2.8. The list goes on for several pages with the cumulative amount becoming larger and larger; when the *cumulative amount* equals the *annual budget*, a line is drawn under that project. For this first pass, those projects *above the line* are tentatively funded; those below it are not, and are tentatively placed on hold.

A second meeting takes place, where managers reconsider the list of projects, particularly those projects close to the line, or those that, perhaps, fall below the line yet might be important ones. Based on management judgement and experience, marginal and other projects can be shifted one way or the other. Also available at this meeting is a breakdown of the funded projects by Product Group, along with the total expected expenditure per Group. This breakdown, together with strategic role and mission of each Group, is used to spot inconsistencies in the resource allocation. For example, if a small business, whose mission is to "maintain and defend", was to receive a high proportion of funded projects and similarly a significant percentage of the total development resources on this first pass, a flag is raised. This Product Group's projects are then reassessed. Ultimately, and after considerable discussion, the final and prioritized list of projects is agreed to.

Exhibit 2.7: The Royal Bank of Canada

Four Decision Criteria in Portfolio Scoring: Operational Definitions

To what extent does the project/product contribute to:

1. Increasing Revenues:

    9 = Excellent revenue generator

    5 = Average revenue generator

    1 = Poor revenue generator

    Weight = 25%

2. Reducing Costs

    9 = Excellent contributor to reducing cost

    5 = Average contributor to reducing cost

    1 = Poor contributor to reducing costs

    Weight = 25%

3. Improving the Quality of the Bank's Financial Portfolio

    9 = Excellent at improving portfolio quality

    5 = Average at improving portfolio quality

    1 = Poor at improving portfolio quality

    Weight = 25%

4. Improving Customer Satisfaction

    9 = Excellent at improving customer satisfaction

    5 = Average at improving customer satisfaction

    1 = Poor at improving customer satisfaction

    Weight = 25%

Exhibit 2.8:   The Royal Bank of Canada – Prioritized List of Projects

Rank Order	Project Name	Project Score (%)	Development Cost (S&T[1] dollars 000) (annual)	Cumulative Development Cost (000)
1	RBCash	83	2,400	2,400
2.	CashCore	76	1,920	4,320
3.	EBX	76	1,800	6,120
4.	EBY	73	500	6,620
5.	BuyAct	73	6,000	12,620
6.	CorpPay	70	2,000	14,620
7.	Project A- PC	70	1,600	16,220
8.	PC-MD	68	7,500	23,720
.	.	.	.	.
.	.	.	.	.
.	.	.	.	.
26.	Tiered/Interest Accounts	55	930	90,150[2]
27	Tiered	52	1,000	
28	Trade-AP	52	1,200	
29	ATM-Y	50	500	
.	.	.	.	.
.	.	.	.	.
.	.	.	.	.

Note: The numbers and names of projects have been disguised.
[1]   S&T: Systems and Technology, analogous to R&D.
[2]   Budget is $90 million; project #26 takes the portfolio slightly over budget. A line is drawn after #26.

Assessment of Scoring Models

Do these scoring model methods work as portfolio management models? There are still some concerns voiced by senior people at Hoechst, Royal Bank and other firms using scoring models; and all confess that some "rough edges" have yet to be ironed out. But overall, users appear to be satisfied with the process and the apparent rigor of their decisions. Managers did express some major concerns with using scoring models as prioritization methods as follows:

1. *Imaginary precision:* While useful, a scoring model should not be over-used nor its results necessarily believed. Certain senior people were concerned that using a scoring model imputed a degree of precision that simply did not exist. As one executive at Hoechst exclaimed: "They're trying to measure a [soft] banana with a micrometer!" Within the gate meetings themselves, there was also evidence of this imaginary precision: for example one project with a score of 49.7% (a fraction below the hurdle of 50%) was allowed to pass; while another with a score of 48.3% was killed. Missing the hurdle by 1.7% was enough to do the project in!

2. *Halo effect:* This was a concern at the Royal Bank of Canada, which over the years has whittled the list of scoring criteria down to the five remaining ones listed above. Why? Management argues that if a project scores high on one criterion, it tends to score high on many of the rest, a halo effect. RBC had started out with a list in excess of 15 criteria, but via statistical analysis[*], showed that this many criteria could be boiled down to a handful of key factors.

3. *Efficiency of allocation of scarce resources:* A final concern is that a missing ingredient in both RBC's and Hoechst's scoring model approaches is to ensure that the resulting list of Go projects indeed achieved the highest possible scores for a given total R&D expenditure. Recall that English China Clay in the ECV approach divided the parameter they were trying to maximize (the project's ECV) by the constraining resource in order to maximize "bang for buck". So did the PI method. The two scoring models shown here fail to do this. For example, one artefact of RBC's scoring scheme is that much larger projects tend to rise to the top of the list; however, if the ranking criterion had been "Project Score/R&D Spend" instead of just "Project Score", then some smaller but efficient projects, requiring much fewer R&D resources, would have risen to the top.

---

[*]   RBC used correlational and factor analysis to reveal that the many scoring criteria they initially used were highly inter-correlated, and could be greatly reduced to a subset of scoring factors.

Summing Up

Four maximization methods have been outlined in this chapter:

1. Expected Commercial Value: A financial method based on a decision tree, incorporating probabilities and resource constraints.

2. Productivity Index: A financial ranking approach using expected commercial value, technical risk and R&D expenditures

3. Dynamic Rank Ordered List: A ranking technique which combines several criteria – NPV, IRR and strategic importance – and ranks projects concurrently on each.

4. Scoring Model: A scoring technique which considers multiple criteria, and combines ratings on these in a weighted fashion to yield an overall or Project Score.

All four have much to commend them. Specific weaknesses – obtaining data, reliability of data, dealing with multiple objectives, imaginary precision, and halo effects – have been outlined throughout the chapter. As a group, their greatest weakness is that they fail to ensure that the portfolio is "on strategy*" or strategically aligned, or that it is even reasonably balanced. For example, the resulting list of projects from any of the methods in this chapter could maximize profits or some project score, but be a very unbalanced list of projects (for example, too many short term ones) or fail to mirror the strategic direction of the business. These are the goals – balance and strategic alignment – that are highlighted in the next two chapters.

In spite of these weaknesses, maximization of the portfolio's value is still a very worthwhile objective. One can argue about balance all one wants and philosophize about strategic direction of the portfolio, but if the projects in the portfolio are poor ones – poor profitability, low likelihoods of success, or poor attractiveness scores – then the portfolio exercise is rather academic. First and foremost, the portfolio must contain "good" projects, and that is where the maximization methods outlined in this chapter excel. One cannot ignore these methods. They must be part of your repertoire of portfolio models.

---

* Although as we shall see in Chapter 4, some firms have modified their scoring models to deal in part with the "on strategy" issue.

Chapter 3

Portfolio Management Methods: A Balanced Portfolio

The second major goal of many firms was the desire to obtain a *balanced portfolio* of new product projects. Their means to achieving this balance varied widely however from company-to-company, and as a result, many different and clever approaches were witnessed. In this chapter we explore the many approaches to portfolio management that can be used to obtain the goal of a balanced portfolio of new products, and we provide some insights into the pros and cons of these methods.

Goal #2: Achieving a Balanced Portfolio

What is a balanced portfolio? It is a balanced set of development projects in terms of a number of key parameters. The analogy is that of an investment fund, where the fund manager seeks balance in terms of high risk versus blue chip stocks, domestic versus foreign investments, and balance across industries in order to arrive at an optimally diversified investment portfolio.

For new product portfolios, the most popular balance tool is the use of various visual charts. Charts are favored for their ability to visually display the balance of projects in the portfolio, something that the lists and scoring models in Chapter 2 failed to do. These visual representations include portfolio maps or bubble diagrams, adaptations of the four-quadrant BCG and McKinsey/GE models. (The latter are the familiar star, cash cow, dog, wildcat models which have seen service as strategy models since the 1970s.) We call these portfolio maps "bubble diagrams" – the description that most people are familiar with – simple because projects are shown as balloons or bubbles. Additionally, visual chart portfolio tools also include traditional histograms and pie charts.

A casual review of portfolio bubble diagrams will lead some to observe that, "these new models are nothing more than the old strategy bubble diagrams of the 70s!". *Not so*. Recall that the BCG strategy model, and others like it (such as the GE and McKinsey models), plotted SBUs on a *market attractiveness* versus *business position* grid. Note that the unit of analysis was the SBU, an existing business – *what is* – whose performance, strengths and weaknesses were all known. By contrast, today's new product portfolio bubble diagrams, while they may appear similar, plot individual *new product projects* – future businesses or *what might be*. As for the dimensions of the grid, there too the "market attractiveness versus business position" dimensions used for existing SBUs may not be as appropriate for new product possibilities; so we saw other dimensions or axes extensively used.

What Dimensions to Consider

What are some of the parameters that companies plot on these bubble diagrams in order to seek balance? Pundits recommend various parameters and lists, and even suggest the "best plots" to use. Here is a sample list of possible parameters to consider; any pair can be the X and Y axes for a bubble plot:

- ▶ fit with business or corporate strategy;
- ▶ inventive merit and strategic importance to the business;
- ▶ durability of the competitive advantage;
- ▶ reward based on financial expectations;
- ▶ competitive impact of technologies (base, key, pacing and embryonic technologies);
- ▶ probabilities of success (technical success and commercial success);
- ▶ R&D costs to completion;
- ▶ time to completion; and,
- ▶ capital and marketing investment required to exploit.[1]

Risk-Reward Bubble Diagrams

Perhaps the most popular bubble diagram is a variant of the risk/return diagram; two different versions are proposed by two consulting firms. Here the horizontal axis is some measure of the reward to the company:

- In ADL's model, as outlined in their book, *Third Generation R&D*, the reward is a qualitative estimate by management ranging from "modest" to "excellent". ADL takes the point of view that too heavy an emphasis on financial analysis can do serious damage, notably in the early stages of a project. Thus reward is a non-quantitative, non-financial metric – a subjective gage of the potential payoffs of the project.[1]

- In contrast, SDG uses a quantitative, financial gauge of reward, namely the shareholder value of the project*.[2]

The vertical axis of both firms' models is the likelihood of success. For ADL, this probability is overall success (probability of *commercial* success times probability of *technical* success); for SDG, probability of *technical* success is the vertical axis, as probability of commercial success has already been built into the shareholder value calculation.

A sample bubble diagram is shown in Exhibit 3.1 for a division of a major chemical company we will call Company T. Note that NPV, adjusted for commercial risks, is the horizontal axis (reverse direction: from right to left); while the vertical axis is the probability of technical success. The size of each bubble shows the annual resources

---

* Shareholder value is the expected commercial value multiplied by the probability of technical success, less expected remaining R&D investment. Uncertain commercial estimates – such as expected sales revenues – have probabilities built in; thus the commercial value has already been discounted for commercial uncertainty.

spent on each project (in Company T's case, this is dollars per year. It could also be FTE* people or work-months allocated to the project).

The four quadrants of the portfolio model are:

▶ *Pearls* (upper left quadrant): These are the potential star products – projects with a high likelihood of success – which are expected to yield very high rewards. Most firms wished they had more of these. Company T has two such Pearl projects, and one of them has been allocated considerable resources (denoted by the sizes of the circles).

▶ *Oysters* (lower left): These are the *long shot* projects – projects with a high expected payoff, but with low likelihood of technical success. They are the projects where technical breakthroughs will pave the way for solid payoffs. Company T has three of these; none is receiving many resources.

▶ *Bread and Butter* (upper right): These are small, simple projects – high likelihood of success, but low reward. They include the extensions, modifications, and up-dating projects. Most companies have too many of these. Company T has a typical over-abundance (note that the large circle here is actually a cluster of related renewal projects). More than 50% of spending goes to these Bread and Butter projects, in Company T's case.

▶ *White Elephants* (lower right): These are the low success probability and low reward projects. Every business has a few white elephants, which inevitably are difficult to kill. Company T has far too many. One third of the projects and about 25% of Company T's spending falls in the lower right White Elephant quadrant.

An attractive feature of this bubble diagram model is that it forces management to deal with the resource issue. Given finite resources (e.g., a limited number of people or money), the sum of the areas of the circles must be a constant. That is, if you add one project to the diagram, you must subtract another; alternatively you can shrink the size of several circles. The elegance here is that the model forces management to consider the resource implications of adding one more project to the list – that some other projects must pay the price!

Also shown in this bubble diagram is the product line with which each project is associated (via the shading or cross-hatching). A final breakdown revealed by Company T via color is timing (although we could not show this with our black and white diagram). Here hot red would mean "imminent launch" while blue means an early stage project. Thus, this apparently simple risk/reward diagram shows a lot more than simply risk and profitability data: It also conveys resource allocation, timing, and allocations across product lines.

---

* FTE: full time equivalent people. This is determined by identifying the number of people on the project team (or helping out) and the percentage of their work-week spent on the project. Often this number was a surprise: a lot of people, but relatively little time spent on any one project!

Exhibit 3.1: Bubble Diagram for Company T: Chemical Company

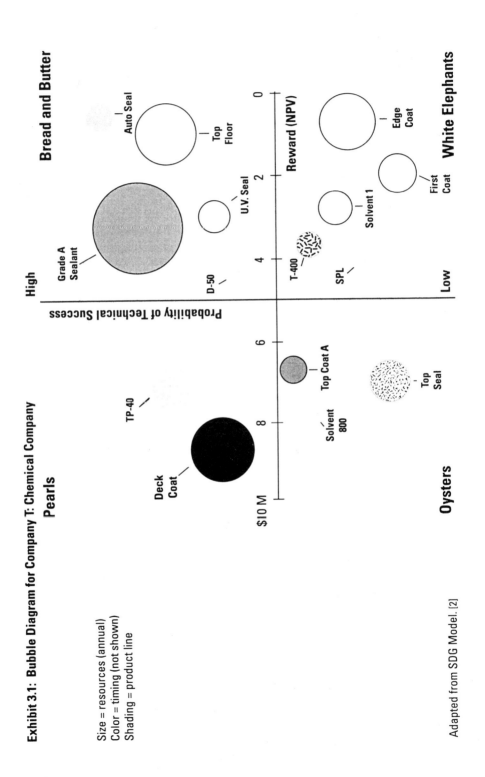

Size = resources (annual)
Color = timing (not shown)
Shading = product line

Adapted from SDG Model. [2]

Using Bubble Diagrams

How is this bubble diagram model used? Unlike the maximization models of Chapter 2, there is no prioritized list of projects produced. Bubble diagrams are very much an *information display* and not so much a *decision model* per se. Nonetheless certain quadrants have more preferred projects than others; and the balance across three of the better quadrants is also vital. From the example in Exhibit 3.1, management debates the appropriateness of the current portfolio and takes necessary action. For example:

- To deal with the overabundance of White Elephants, the company initiated an immediate review of these five projects with the idea of pruning the list and re-allocating resources to more deserving projects. Note that there were a number of fairly good projects on hold awaiting resources (these are not shown on the bubble diagram, but one company we interviewed also produced a bubble diagram of the "on hold" projects).

- Management felt that the three Oyster projects were about the right number, but decided to increase resources here to move them along more quickly. Two in particular were starved for resources.

- Projects in the upper right quadrant – the Bread and Butter ones, accounting for more than 50% of spending – were closely scrutinized. There was a general unease on the part of senior management about the high level of spending here (the business had been designated a "growth business"). There was also a concern about whether they were in danger of becoming "busy fools" – a lot of activity around a number of trivial projects. As a result, several were cancelled or postponed.

- Several projects in the Hold Vault were immediately activated (projects which had been placed on Hold due to lack of resources – no people to work on them). People resources were made available by cutting back on the White Elephants and Bread and Butter projects.

Bubble diagrams found use in two settings. The first and most obvious was in portfolio review meetings, much like the situation described at Company T. Here the entire portfolio of projects is periodically reviewed – for example, semi-annually or quarterly – and appropriate actions are taken, as described above. The second use of bubble diagrams – and indeed all the visual charts in this chapter – was at gate review meetings. At these meetings, the project under consideration was shown on a bubble diagram, which displayed other projects on hold awaiting resources - and was compared to others in the queue. Additionally, the bubble diagram of active projects would also be displayed to portray how the proposed project might fit into the total portfolio of active projects. Note that various software packages have been developed to assist in the construction of bubble diagrams.

Variants of Risk-Reward Bubble Diagrams

<u>Dealing With Commercial Risks</u>: One problem with the bubble diagram employed by Company T is that it requires a point estimate of the reward, namely the likely or probable NPV. Technical risks are captured by the vertical axis, namely probability of technical success, but not so for the commercial risks. Some businesses at 3M use a variant of the bubble diagram which portrays uncertainties. In calculating the NPV, high and low estimates are made for uncertain variables. This leads to high/low case NPV estimates for each project. Similarly high/low estimates are made for the probability of technical success. The result is shown in Exhibit 3.2. The size of bubbles or balloons on the portfolio map thus capture uncertainty of projects. Here, very small bubbles mean highly certain estimates on each dimension, whereas large bubbles or ellipses mean considerable uncertainty (a high spread between worst case and best case) for that project.[3] (Note: The ellipse reflects an approximately 80% chance that the value of the project falls within the ellipse with no implied probability difference.)

Exhibit 3.2: Bubble Diagram – R&D Portfolio Example

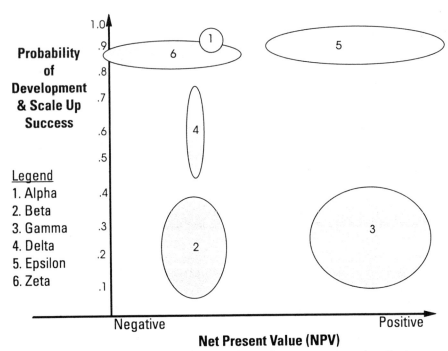

Note: Larger circles and ellipses denote more uncertain estimates.

Adapted from "New Produce Investment Portfolio" by Dr. Gary L. Tritle. [3]

<u>Non financial rewards</u>: Some pundits argue that strict reliance on financial estimates can do considerable damage; that low risk, simple "low hanging fruit" projects will be favored while strategically important or potential breakthrough projects will fare less well. Sometimes strategic issues and the quest for significant projects must take precedence over strictly financial and short term return. Moreover, financial data is very often highly unreliable, especially in the pre-development stages, where the portfolio is being decided. And portfolio models, where one axis is the NPV, assume a level of precision of financial data far beyond what most project teams can provide. A proposed alternative is to use a non-financial measure of reward: this is a subjective estimate ranging from "modest" to "excellent" and depends not only on the financial prospects for the project, but also its strategic importance and impact on the company. Conveniently, both probabilities – commercial success and technical success – are incorporated into the vertical axis, as shown in Exhibit 3.3.[1]

Exhibit 3.3: Bubble Diagram with Non-Financial Measures

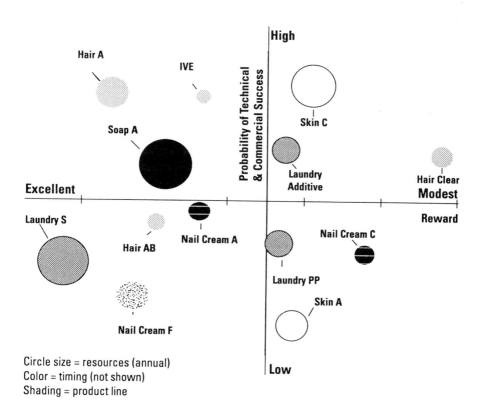

Circle size = resources (annual)
Color = timing (not shown)
Shading = product line

Source: Based on ADL model. [1]

A Simpler Portfolio Map

A somewhat simpler illustration of the risk-reward diagram is provided by Reckitt & Colman, as one of the many visual charts that comprise their portfolio model.

> Reckitt & Colman (R&C) is a major multinational producer of frequently purchased household consumer goods and pharmaceutical products. Headquartered in London, England, the firm's products are found in most countries worldwide under a variety of brand names. In North America, familiar brands sold by R&C include Easy-Off oven cleaner, Air Wick air freshener, Lysol disinfectant cleaners, and Woolite fabric wash. R&C's worldwide sales revenues are in excess of $4 billion (US).

Reckitt & Colman portrays the portfolio of projects on a much less complex portfolio map diagram than Company T. Here the NPV is plotted against the overall probability of success, as shown in Exhibit 3.4. The various types of projects are also shown on the diagram: new business (new products in a new category), new products and product improvements. Thus, two elements of balance are revealed in a single diagram: risk-reward and project type.

Exhibit 3.4: Reckitt & Colman – Probability of Success vs. NPV

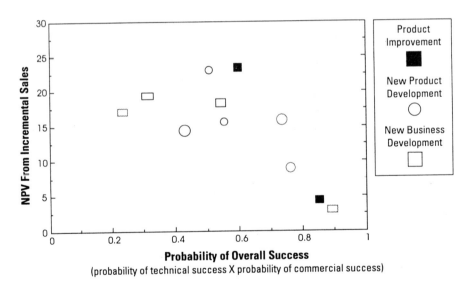

Probability of Overall Success
(probability of technical success X probability of commercial success)

Note: This chart is an illustration of the type of additional information available at Portfolio Reviews at R&C.

Here, the probability of overall success (horizontal axis) is simply the two probabilities – technical and commercial success - multiplied together. And the NPV considers only incremental sales (i.e., cannibalized sales are subtracted).

Scoring Models and Bubble Diagrams

A combined scoring model and bubble diagram is used by Specialty Minerals, a spin-off company of Pfizer. The scoring model (see Chapter 2) considers seven factors, to construct a rank ordered list of projects:

- ► Management Interest*
- ► Customer Interest
- ► Sustainability of Competitive Advantage
- ► Technical Feasibility
- ► Business Case Strength
- ► Fit with Core Competencies
- ► Profitability and Impact.

These same factors are also used to construct a bubble diagram (not shown):

Vertical axis: Probability of success, consisting of a weighted combination of Customer Interest, Technical Feasibility and Fit with Core Competencies.

Horizontal axis: Value to the company, consisting of a weighted combination of Profitability and Competitive Advantage.

The novel feature in this company's approach is the use of a hybrid model (a scoring model and a bubble diagram), both of which make use of the same factors.

Factoring Risk into the Value Calculation

Frequently, in the companies we studied, the reward of the project was captured on the portfolio map or bubble diagram by the NPV. Both Company T and Reckitt & Colman used NPV in their bubble diagrams, as was the case in many other firms we visited. The issue of how to calculate the NPV was a common concern, however. Different models and different firms treated risk in a variety of ways in this NPV calculation:

- Build probabilities right into the NPV calculation: Company G, which used the Dynamic Rank Ordered list in Chapter 2, also displayed portfolio maps similar to those in this chapter. This company simply factored down all uncertain estimates in the NPV calculation by their probability of occurring. For example, if projected revenues were uncertain, the Finance Department would multiply these by a probability of 0.80, or perhaps 0.60, to account for that uncertainty. Mathematically, this procedure is not strictly correct, but it did serve to dramatically scale back wildly optimistic financial projections.

- Use risk adjusted discount rates: Company T used variable discount rates when it calculated the NPV. In effect, these were risk adjusted discount rates. For example, new product projects whose commercial projections were highly uncertain used a discount rate of *double the risk free hurdle rate*. Low risk projects, such as

---

* Modified from Specialty Minerals exact list.

product modifications and renewals or process improvements, used a discount rate of 1.5 times the risk free hurdle rate, and so on. What this procedure does is penalize higher risk projects – their NPV is scaled back accordingly.

- Use a Monte Carlo simulation: Company M, a medical products firm, used a portfolio model similar to Company T's in Exhibit 3.1. The probability of technical success was taken into account on the vertical axis, but the probability of commercial success was not. To account for commercial uncertainty, every variable required three estimates: high, low and likely*. So, revenue, costs, launch timing and so on each had three estimates provided by the project team. From these three estimates, a *probability distribution curve* was determined for each variable. Next, random scenarios were generated for the project using these probability curves as variable inputs. Thousands of scenarios were computer-generated (hence the name Monte Carlo – thousand of spins of the wheel), and the result was a distribution of financial outcomes. From this, the expected NPV was determined – an NPV figure with all commercial outcomes and their probabilities figured in. This is an interesting technique, and a mathematically elegant one. Management at Company M was strongly endorsing the rigorous method; but it was proving to be a significant burden to the project teams who were asked to supply an endless stream of data! Moreover, private conversations with team members revealed that they simply did not have the data required, and that they were providing the "model owner" with nonsense data – largely invented numbers. Even with this fault, however, the Monte Carlo approach was found to be useful by a number of other companies; for example, Procter & Gamble which employed a version of Monte Carlo simulation called "At Risk"; and Nova Chemicals in Canada.

- Decision tree: The Expected Commercial Value (ECV) method, used by ECC International, was based on a simple decision tree (see Chapter 2). It appropriately incorporated the future stream of earnings, various capital and development costs incurred throughout the project, and the probabilities of technical and commercial success. The computation was relatively straightforward and the ECV certainly can be used here in various bubble diagrams. Based on its success at ECC, we recommend having a close look at the ECV method as one way to build risk into the NPV calculation.

- High Case/Low Case: This method, used at 3M and described earlier in this chapter, captures uncertainties on both risk and reward dimensions of the bubble diagram by using "high" and "low" case scenarios. The size and shape of the bubble denotes the uncertainty or risk associated with each project (see Exhibit 3.2).

- Simple probabilities: Recall that the ADL bubble diagram model (shown in Exhibit 3.3) relies on a non-financial measure of reward (above) and does not use a NPV calculation per se. Realistically, however, the NPV is hard to ignore when assessing the projects's potential reward to the company. There is no need to build in probabilities or uncertainties into this reward metric, however, because both probabilities (commercial and technical success) are combined into an overall probability of success on the vertical axis (see Exhibit 3.3).

---

* The 10%, 50% and 90% points on the probability distribution curve.

More Portfolio Maps: Ease Versus Attractiveness

Other very useful variants of bubble diagrams portray the portfolio of projects in a number of relevant ways. A most useful portfolio map at Reckitt & Colman, in management's view, is their Ease versus Attractiveness chart. Here the axes are Market/Concept Attractiveness and Ease of Implementation (see Exhibit 3.5). Both axes in Exhibit 3.5 are constructed from multi-item 1-5 scales, which are added in a weighted fashion. These two axes are defined in Exhibit 3.6.

A second and parallel bubble diagram plots Market/Concept Attractiveness (defined in Exhibit 3.6) versus Financial Attractiveness (see bubble diagram in Exhibit 3.7). The latter axis is based on a NPV calculation.

Exhibit 3.5: Reckitt & Colman – Market/Concept Attractiveness vs. Ease of Implementation

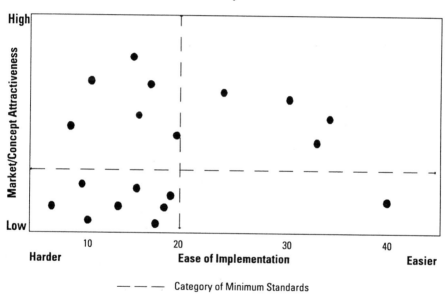

— — — Category of Minimum Standards

Both axes are based on a weighted addition of multiple items (much like a scoring model) – see Exhibit 3.6.

Black circles represent a new product project.

Exhibit 3.6: Reckitt & Colman – Definitions of Market/Concept Attractiveness and Ease of Implementation

Items Comprising Market/Concept Attractiveness Score (Vertical Axis)		
Factor	Weighting	Five Point Scale (1-5)
Purchase Intent	5	1. Significantly below average. 2. Slightly below average. 3. Equal to average. 4. Slightly above average. 5. Significantly above average.
Advantage Over What's Available	5	1. Significantly below average. 2. Slightly below average. 3. Equal to average. 4. Slightly above average. 5. Significantly above average.
Performance in Use	5	1. Little prospect of performance advantage. 2. Uncertain prospect of performance advantage. 3. Some prospects for slight advantage. 4. Some prospects for important product advantage. 5. Good prospects for important product advantage.
Competitive Position Improvement	2.5	1. Helps to modernize brand, but doesn't enhance franchise long-term. 2. Contributes to brand's strategic plan & helps to make franchise contempary. 3. Contributes to brand's strategic plan & keeps franchise contempary. 4. Builds brand and franchise long term. 5. Significantly builds brand and franchise long term.
Sustainability of Competitive Advantage	2.5	1. <6 months 2. 6-12 months 3. 1-2 years 4. 2-5 years 5. >5 years
Geographic Scope*	2.5	1. Local project - developed market. 2. Local project - developing market. 3. Regional project - developed market. 4. Regional project - developing market. 5. Multi-regional project.

Note: The Market Attractiveness of a project is the weighted summation of scores on the items above.
* R&C divided the world into regions: Europe, North America, Central/South America, Pacific and so on. A "regional project" accommodates multiple countries, e.g. Europe. A "local" project is one country.

Continued...

Exhibit 3.6 continued:
Reckitt & Colman – Definitions of Market/Concept Attractiveness and Ease of Implementation

Items Comprising Ease of Implementation Score (Horizontal Axis)		
Factor	**Weighting**	**Scale**
Technical Competitive Strength	4.5	1. Weak 2. Tenable 3. Favourable 4. Strong 5. Dominant
Technical Maturity	9	1. Embryonic 2. Growth 3. Mature 4. Aging
Registration/ Clinical Trial	4.5	1. Major problems are anticipated in most markets. 2. Major problems are anticipated in some markets. 3. Minor problems are anticipated. 4. No problems are anticipated. 5. No registration or clinical trial required.
Packaging Components	3	1. Needs basic advances in packaging technology. 2. Several new components need development. 3. A new component needs development. 4. Needs modifications to existing components. 5. Uses existing components.
Manufacture	3	1. Needs basic advances in manufacturing technology. 2. Needs new manufacturing equipment (>100,000). 3. Needs major modifications (<100,000) or use of copacker. 4. Needs minor modifications (<25,000). 5. Uses existing manufacturing equipment.
Sales & Distribution	3	1. New sales/buyer skills needed in new distribution channel. 2. Existing sales skills in new distribution channel. 3. New skills required by both salespeople & buyers. 4. Some new skills required. 5. No change necessary to existing sales effort.

Note: The Ease of Implementation of a project is the weighted summation of scores on the items above.

Exhibit 3.7: Reckitt & Colman – Financial Attractiveness vs. Market/Concept Attractiveness

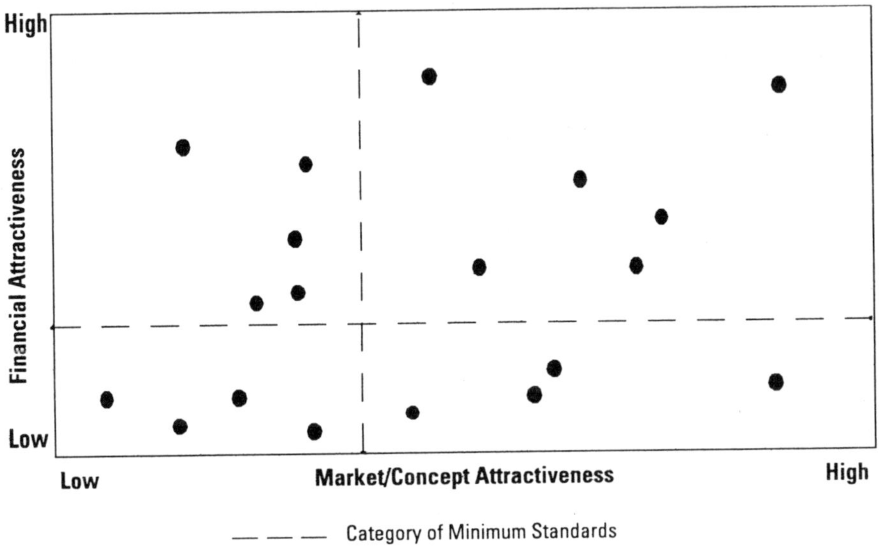

— — — Category of Minimum Standards

Using the Ease vs. Attractiveness Portfolio Map

R&C's portfolio maps are used much the same way that Company T uses its bubble diagram: Managers look for projects in favorable quadrants (towards the upper right of the diagram in Exhibit 3.5), scrutinize those in the "unattractive and hard-to-do" quadrant, and look for balance between ease and attractiveness. For example in Exhibit 3.5:

- There is a surprising shortage of easy-to-do projects. This is a departure from the plethora of "low hanging fruit" projects the company typically focused on only a few years ago. Perhaps the pendulum has swung too much the other way and a better balance should be sought between easy and challenging projects. Therefore, management would be looking for an increase in the number of easier projects.

- There are clearly too few projects in the desirable upper right quadrant. One outcome of this analysis is a recognition of the need for increased focus on idea/concept generation and the need to move far more concepts through the early phase screening. Further, while resource allocations are not shown on the diagram, clearly resource commitments for the three potential stars is an issue.

- With eight projects out of 19 in the lower left quadrant (more difficult and less attractive), management must ask some very tough questions: Why are there so many projects here? Which ones should be cancelled? What is the rationale for each? (Perhaps there are strategic, competitive or defensive reasons for doing these.) How much are we spending this year on projects in this quadrant? (Perhaps management can postpone a few to reduce resource commitment here.) And, can some of the better ones be made more attractive or easier to do by changing the definition, scope, resource commitment or plan of action?

- Another six projects are in the attractive but hard-to-do quadrant. Again, vital questions about these six must focus on ways to improve their ease of implementation. For example, by increasing resource commitments, can some of the technical, manufacturing and packaging barriers be overcome?

Other Bubble Charts

There are numerous parameters, dimension or variables across which one might wish to seek a balance of projects. As a result, an endless variety of X-Y plots or bubble diagrams is possible[1].

Market and Technology Risk

Should all projects be low risk to the company? Exhibit 3.8 portrays projects in terms of both technology risk and market risk. Once again a balance is sought.

Exhibit 3.8: Market and Technology Risk Bubble Diagram

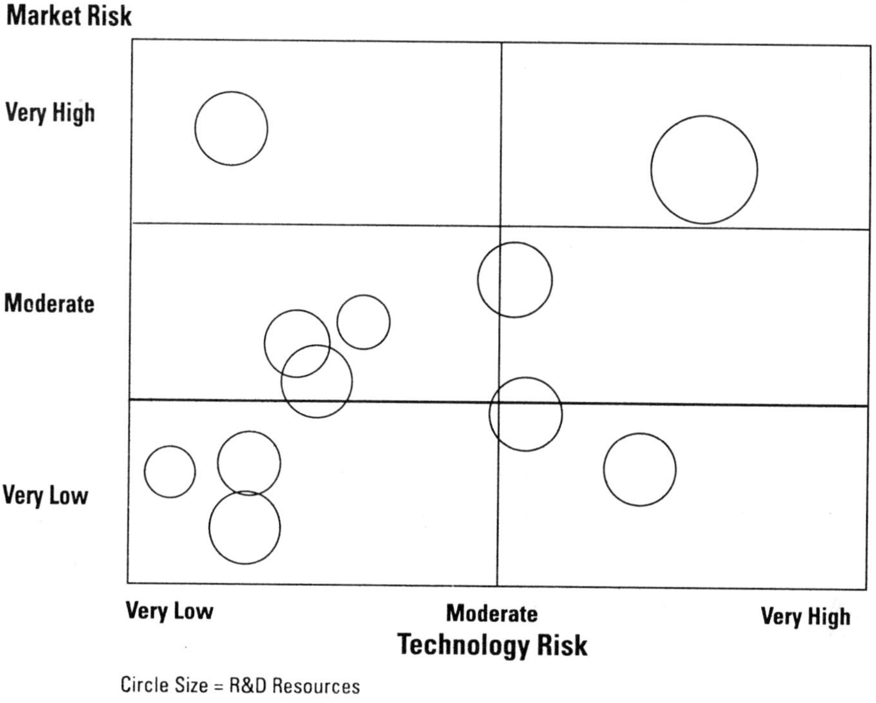

Market Risk

Circle Size = R&D Resources

Three Dimensional Diagrams

Procter & Gamble is experimenting with a novel 3-dimensional plot, made possible via CAD software. (Our Exhibit 3.9, on two dimensional paper, does not do the model justice!) Here, time-to-market, NPV and Probability of Commercial Success are the three axes. The model can be rotated in 3-dimensional space to provide various views.

Exhibit 3.9: P&G Three Dimensional Bubble Diagram

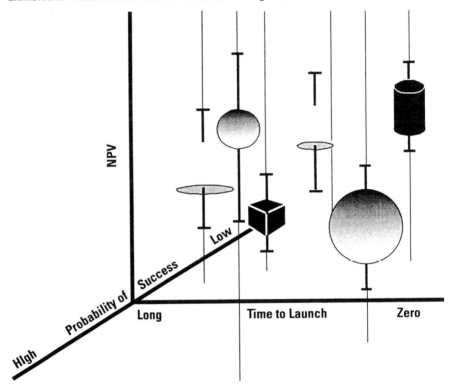

The three axes are:
X = Time to Launch date
Y = NPV
Z = Probability of Commercial Success

Shapes denote degree of technological fit with company (spheres are high; cubes low).

I-bars denote range of NPV (based on Monte Carlo Simulation)

Exhibit 3.9: Three-dimensional portfolio model, as used in Procter & Gamble's Corporate New Ventures Group (developed by Tom Chorman, Finance Manager, CNV, P&G)

Other Types of Charts

Other types of charts – histograms and pie charts – effectively capture numerous other parameters, across which one seeks to attain balance.

Capacity Utilization

What proportion of allocated or budgeted resources are projects actually using? Often there are gaps between actual and proposed spending. Exhibit 3.10 shows an example. This is a useful chart when discussing the resource allocation issue in a portfolio review.

Exhibit 3.10: Capacity Utilization

Project Name

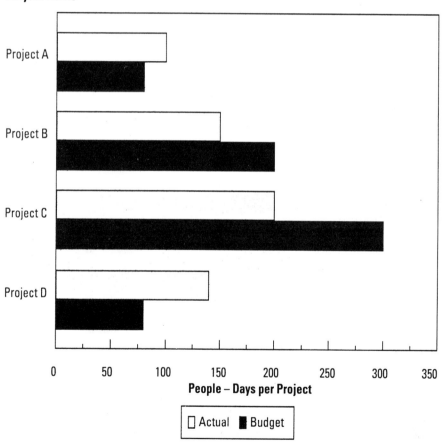

Project Timing

Timing is a key issue in the quest for portfolio balance. One does not wish to invest 100% in either short or long-term projects. Another timing goal is for a steady stream of new product launches spread out over the years – constant "new news" with no sudden log-jam of product launches all in one year. The histogram in Exhibit 3.11 captures the issue of timing and portrays the distribution of resources to specific projects according to years of launch. For example, for Company T, 35% of monies are allocated to four projects – all due to be launched within the year (year 1). Another 30% of resources are being spent on four projects whose projected launch date is the following year (year 2), and so on.

Exhibit 3.11: Timing of Product Launches

% of Resources (this year)

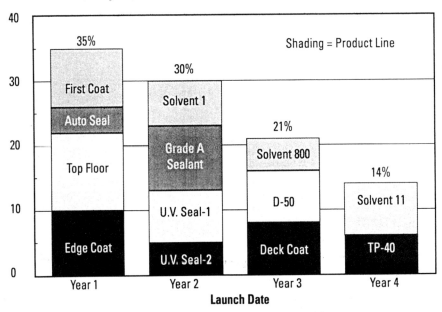

Another timing issue is cash flow. Here the desire is to balance projects in such a way that cash inflows are reasonably balanced with cash outflows. For example, one might wish to avoid the situation where, when all projects are considered together, there are huge cash outflows in one year and huge cash inflows several years later. Reckitt & Colman produces a histogram that captures the total cash flow per year for all projects in the portfolio (Exhibit 3.12). This histogram also reveals cash flows by project type.

Exhibit 3.12: Reckitt & Colman – Cash Flow vs. Time

'000

Note: This chart is an illustration of the type of additional information available.
Numbers have been disguised for each year.

Project Types

Project types is yet another vital concern. What is the spending on genuine new products versus updates versus fundamental research? And what should it be? Pie or similar type charts, which capture the spending split across project types, were found in just about every company we studied. Exhibit 3.13 provides an illustration.

Exhibit 3.13: Spending Allocation Across Project Types

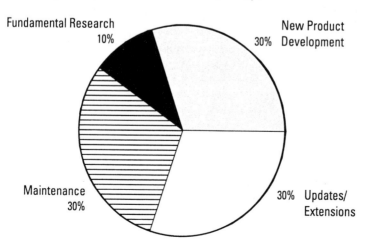

Markets, Products & Technologies

Another set of dimensions across which managers sought balance was product, market and technology type. Exhibit 3.14 provides a sample visual breakdown demonstrating how a niche chemical company divided its product lines and markets using pie charts. The question was: Do we have the appropriate split in R&D spending across our various product lines? Or across the markets or market segments in which we compete? Or across the technologies we posses? Pie charts are an excellent approach for capturing and displaying this type of data.

Exhibit 3.14: Breakdown of Resources by Product Lines & Markets

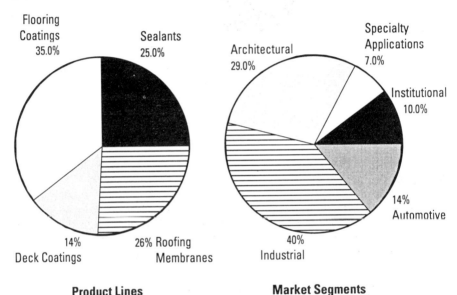

Product Lines

Market Segments

Balance: Critical Comments

There is much to be said for achieving the right balance of projects in the product development portfolio. That is, there is more to life than simply achieving a high value portfolio; balance is also a critical issue. The trouble is that achieving balance – or selecting an appropriate tool to help achieve balance – is easier conceptually than in practice.

What impressed us was how many intricate and ingenious methods and diagrams companies had invented to deal with this balance issue. We could have filled an entire book with the maps, bubble diagrams and pie charts we discovered in our study. In spite of all this cleverness, however, there remain problems with the quest for balance:

1.   First, some of the more popular bubble diagrams suffered the same fate as the maximization models outlined in Chapter 2: They rely on substantial financial

data, when often this financial data is either unavailable or, at best, highly uncertain. Witness the popular risk-reward bubble diagrams (Exhibit 3.1, 3.2 and 3.4) where NPV is one of the axes.

2. Second, there is the issue of information overload. "Maps, endless maps!" was the complaint of one exasperated executive, as he leafed through more than a dozen maps plotting everything versus everything in his firm's portfolio model. Conversely, very few companies had even attempted to use all the maps and charts recommended by the various pundits.

3. Third, these models are information display, not decision models per se. Unlike the value maximization methods of Chapter 2, the result is not a magic list of preferred projects. Rather, these charts and maps are a starting point for discussion only. Management still has to translate this data into actionable decisions. Some had failed here. Too many maps, or the wrong maps, may have contributed.

4. Fourth, it wasn't clear what the "right balance" of projects was. Management could stare all they wanted at various charts, but unless a portfolio is obviously and extremely out-of-balance (as in Company T's Exhibit 3.1), how does a manager know whether the right balance is there? For example, one portfolio manager at Hewlett-Packard speculated about the optimal balance of projects – about whether there might be any "rules of thumb" about the best split in long term versus short term projects, high risk versus low risk, and so on – much like rules of thumb exist in stock market investment portfolios. If one lacks an idea of what the right balance is in the first place – the *what should be* – then all these balance maps and charts – the *what is* – are meaningless. What is the existing balance being compared against?

5. Finally, it wasn't clear in all cases how the charts and maps were actually used. At Reckett & Colman, the initial inclination was to make these part of gate meetings. After a few attempts, this practice was halted because it added to the confusion. The company has since worked out a better method of integrating portfolio and gate decisions, which we will see in Chapter 5. At the Royal Bank of Canada, electronic portfolio maps* were also used at gate meetings, but only a few times before they, too, gave up. Company G used the maps as an after-the-fact course correction – "to make sure we have the right balance". But it was never clear what would happen if the "wrong balance" ever occurred: would management immediately start cancelling projects, and approving others in the hold tank?

The fact that portfolio balance methods are far from perfect does not mean we suggest they be dismissed outright. *Certainly not!* But such methods should be used

---

* The Royal Bank of Canada developed computer generated graphics displaying the entire portfolio on a bubble diagram via a video projector for use at gate meetings. Simply by clicking the mouse, projects could be made to disappear or re-appear; and resources could be allocated from one project to another (the circles changed in size). This was all very clever, but it did not suit the gate meeting well.

with care; the choice of maps (which axes to use in the plots, for example) and charts (which parameters to show) must be well thought out. One must avoid the temptation to portray too many maps and charts, and one must be sure to test the maps in portfolio or gate meetings before adopting them.

One added benefit of the various balancing charts and maps is that they connect very well with the methods used to achieve the other two goals in portfolio management. Portfolio maps, for example, provide inputs into maximizing the portfolio value against goals (Chapter 2). In one firm, projects which scored high on the risk and reward matrix were flagged for priority. These projects, if successful, would help the company achieve its goals of increasing the average margin of its portfolio of products on the market.

Portfolio maps can also be used as an effective aid in monitoring a firm's portfolio versus its strategy. In other words, maps can serve as a tool for monitoring to ensure that the portfolio is in line with the strategy. If not, then course corrections can be made periodically during the year. The next chapter explores this third goal of portfolio management – the strategy link – in more depth.

Chapter 4

Portfolio Management Methods: A Strong Link to Strategy

Goal #3: The Need to Build Strategy into the Portfolio

Strategy and resource allocation must be intimately connected. Strategy begins when you start spending money! Until one begins allocating resources to specific activities – for example, to specific development projects – strategy is just words in a strategy document. These were the views shared by enlightened management of the companies we investigated. In some firms the prime focus was on ensuring that:

►   active projects were "on strategy"; and that
►   resource allocations truly reflected the desired strategic direction of the business.

The mission, vision and strategy of the business must be operationalized in terms of where the business spends money. Well-meaning words are worthless without the resource commitments to back them up. For example, if a business's strategic mission is to "grow via leading edge product development", then this must be reflected in the number of new product projects underway – projects that will lead to growth (rather than simply defend the status quo) and projects that really are innovative. Similarly, if the strategy is to focus on certain markets, products or technology types, then the majority of R&D spending must be focused on such markets, products or technologies. After all, isn't this what strategy is all about: to guide the actions and efforts of the business?

Not every company we studied had achieved proficiency here. For example, one business unit's senior executive claimed that "my SBU's strategy is to achieve rapid growth through product leadership"; yet when we examined his SBU's breakdown of R&D spending, the great majority of resources was going to maintenance projects, product modifications and extensions. Clearly this was a case of a disconnect between *stated strategy* and *where the money is spent*. This executive was not alone!

Linking Strategy to the Portfolio: Approaches

Two broad objectives arise in the desire to build in strategy and to achieve *strategic alignment* in portfolio management:

•   The first addresses this question: Do all our projects fit strategically; that is, are they consistent with our business's strategy? For example, if we have defined certain technologies or markets as key areas to focus on, do our projects fit into these areas – are they in bounds or out of bounds?

- The second is more difficult and addresses this question: Does the break-down of our spending reflect our strategic priorities? That is, if we say we are a growth business, then the majority of our R&D spending ought to be in projects that are designed to grow the business. In short, when we add up the areas where we are spending money, are these totals consistent with our stated strategy? Often the answer is no, so there are serious disconnects.

Two general approaches to deal with strategic alignment were observed in the companies we studied:

- Building strategic criteria into project selection tools: Here strategic fit was achieved simply by incorporating numerous strategic criteria into the Go/Kill and prioritization methods; and

- Top-down strategy models, which began with the business's strategy and then moved to setting aside funds – envelopes or buckets of money – destined for different types of projects.

Strategic Criteria Built into Project Selection Tools

A popular project selection method is the use of a scoring model (Chapter 2). Scoring models can help achieve two key portfolio goals, namely ensuring the strategic fit of projects, as well as maximizing the value of the portfolio (as seen in Chapter 2). One of the multiple objectives considered in a scoring model – along with profitability or likelihood of success – can be to *maximize strategic fit*. The way to achieve this is to build into the scoring model a number of strategic questions.

An example:
In the scoring model used by Hoechst (Exhibit 2.6), forty percent of the major factors – two major factors out of five – are strategic. Of the 19 criteria used to prioritize projects, six or almost one-third deal with strategic issues. Thus, projects which fit the firm's strategy and boast strategic leverage are likely to rise to the top of the list. Indeed, it is inconceivable how "off strategy" projects could make the active list at all; the scoring model naturally weeds them out.

Another example:
Reckett & Colman subjects all projects to a list of "Must" criteria at gates before any prioritization consideration is given. At the top of this list is the Must criterion – *strategic fit*. Projects which fail this criterion are knocked out immediately. Next a set of "Should Meet" criteria is used via a scoring model. Unless the project scores a certain minimum point count, again, it is knocked out. Embedded within this scoring model are several strategic direction criteria. For example, Reckitt & Colman's strategy calls for more international products (and fewer domestically-oriented developments); hence this international criterion is one of the scoring criteria, so that projects that are international receive more points. In this way, the portfolio over time will deliberately be biased towards international projects. Finally, in R&C's bubble diagram (where Attractiveness

is plotted versus Ease - see Exhibit 3.5), of the six parameters which make up Attractiveness, two capture important strategic directions:

▶ competitive position improvement (ability to build the brand and franchise in the long term); and

▶ geographic scope (international projects favored).

Thus Reckitt & Colman builds in strategic fit and direction throughout its scoring and bubble diagram portfolio approaches.

The scoring model approach is recommended for two reasons. First, it is quite simple to use and understand. Second, it kills two birds with one stone: Scoring models are appropriate techniques to achieve maximization of key variables (including financial), and at the same time can be used to ensure strategic fit.

The only weakness is that *only one half of the strategic goal is achieved*, namely ensuring that all projects are "on strategy". What scoring models do not do is ensure that the spending breakdown in the portfolio (where the money is spent) reflects the strategic priorities of the business. In short, all projects may be on strategy, but the balance or *split of resource spending* may be wrong. For example, there may be too many projects in one strategic market and not enough in another. This shortfall leads logically to the second strategic method, which establishes buckets of resources.

Top Down Strategic Approaches

A top down approach is the only method we observed that is designed to ensure the eventual portfolio of projects truly reflects the stated (or desired) strategy for each business unit: that where the money is spent mirrors the business's strategy. There were several variants of this approach.

Strategic Buckets Model

This top down method operates from the simple principle that *implementing strategy equates to spending money on specific projects* (or put another way, "strategy is not real until it translates into spending money on specific activities or projects"). Thus, setting portfolio requirements really means "setting spending targets". A number of firms we studied used bits and pieces of this approach. What we describe below is a composite of several companies' methods.

The approach begins with the business's strategy and requires senior management to make forced choices along each of several dimensions – choices about how they wish to allocate their scarce money resources. This enables the creation of "envelopes of money" or "buckets". Existing projects are sorted into buckets; then, one determines whether actual spending is consistent with desired spending. Finally, projects are prioritized within buckets to arrive at the ultimate portfolio of projects: one that mirrors management's desired strategy. Several companies were using variants of this method.

Here are the key steps:

1. A vision and strategy for the business are first developed. This includes defining strategic goals and the general plan of attack to achieve these goals – a fairly standard business strategy exercise.

2. Forced choices are made across key strategic dimensions. That is, based on this strategy, the management of the business allocates R&D and other resources (either in dollars or as a percent) across categories in each dimension. Some dimensions which we witnessed included:

   ▸ Strategic goals: Management is forced to split resources across the specified strategic goals. For example, what percent (or how many dollars) should be spent on Defending the Base; on Diversifying; on Extending the Base? and so on.

   ▸ Product lines: Resources are split across product lines. For example, how much to spend on Product Line A? On Product Line B? On C? The stage of the product life cycle of each line's market should influence this split.

   ▸ Project types: What percent of resources should go to new product development? To maintenance-type projects? To process improvements? To fundamental research? etc.

   One business within Exxon Chemical uses the Product/Market Newness diagram illustrated in Exhibit 4.1 to visualize this split across project types. Here, the six different types of projects each received a certain percentage of the total budget.

   ▸ Familiarity Matrix: What should be the split of resources to different types of markets and to different technology types in terms of their *familiarity to the business*? Some firms used the "familiarity matrix" proposed by Roberts, where both markets and technologies are categorized into three types (see Exhibit 4.2*):
   - existing markets (or technologies) for the company;
   - extensions of current markets (or technologies); and,
   - new markets (or technologies) for the company.

   Eastman Chemical uses a four-cell version of this matrix (Exhibit 4.2) to allocate resources into buckets; Dow Corning uses a nine-cell matrix.

   ▸ Geography: What proportion of resources should be spent on projects aimed largely at North America? At Latin America? At Europe? At the Pacific? Or aimed globally?

---

* See Roberts.[1] Note that the Roberts familiarity matrix (Exhibit 4.2) is somewhat different than the one used by Exxon in Exhibit 4.1. In the Roberts matrix's, both dimensions are "newness to the company"; whereas, in the Categories of New Products matrix, originally proposed by Booz-Allen & Hamilton, one dimension captures newness to the company, the other newness to the market. These are subtle but very important differences, and they lead to quite different definitions of projects within each cell.

Exhibit 4.1: Six Project Categories (used in a SBU in Exxon Chemical).

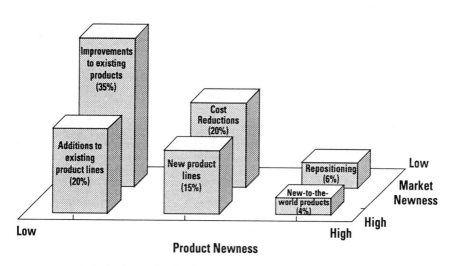

Note: Each type of project is represented by a box on the chart.

Exhibit 4.2: Familiarity Matrix – Technology and Market Newness

Technology Newness	Market Newness	
	Existing/Base	**New**
New Step Out	Step Out Product Development	New Businesses & New Ventures (step out projects)
New But Familiar	New Items (existing lines)	Market Development
Base	Defend and/or Penetrate	Market Expansion (customer application projects)

3. Strategic buckets are defined. Here the various strategic dimensions (above) are collapsed into a convenient handful of buckets (see Exhibit 4.3). For example:
    ▸ Product Development Projects for Product Lines A & B;
    ▸ Cost Reduction Projects for all products;
    ▸ Product Renewal Projects for Product Lines C & D; and so on.

4. Current spending in each bucket is determined. This is a relatively simple accounting exercise of categorizing on-going projects by bucket, and adding up annual spending on each project within a given bucket.

5. Desired spending by bucket is determined. This involves a consolidation of the "what is" information from item 4 above with the "what should be" from the strategic allocation exercise in items 2 and 3 above.

6. Gaps are identified. This step compares the actual spending per bucket (item 4 above) with the desired spending (item 5). Differences between the two levels are identified as gaps.

7. Projects within each bucket are rank-ordered. Companies use either scoring models or financial criteria here (see Exhibit 4.3).

Exhibit 4.3: Projects Prioritized Within Strategic Buckets

New Products: Product Line A Target Spend: $8.7M	New Products: Product Line B Target Spend: $18.5M	Maintenance of Business: Product Lines A & B Target Spend: $10.8M	Cost Reductions: All Products Target Spend: $7.8M
Project A 4.1	Project B 2.2	Project E 1.2	Project I 1.9
Project C 2.1	Project D 4.5	Project G 0.8	Project M 2.4
Project F 1.7	Project K 2.3	Project H 0.7	Project N 0.7
Project L 0.5	Project T 3.7	Project J 1.5	Project P 1.4
Project X 1.7	**Gap = 5.8**	Project Q 4.8	Project S 1.6
Project Y 2.9		Project R 1.5	Project U 1.0
Project Z 4.5		Project V 2.5	Project AA 1.2
Project BB 2.6		Project W 2.1	

Projects rank ordered within columns according to a financial criterion: NPV x Probability of Success; or ECV; or a scoring model (Chapter 2).

8. Adjustments are made. Where overspending occurs within a bucket – for example, too many renewal-type projects – projects can be pruned; or, as most companies did, management gives proportionately fewer approvals for up-coming projects of this type. Conversely, where underspending is occurring – for example, not enough genuine new product projects for product line then management encourages more such projects, and may even relax some of the Go/Kill gating criteria here.

Over time, the portfolio of projects, and the spending across strategic buckets, will eventually equal management's desired spending levels across buckets. At this point, the portfolio of projects truly mirrors the strategy for the business.

Strategic Buckets: Strengths & Weaknesses

Of all the attempts to build strategy into the portfolio selection process, top down approaches such as the Strategic Buckets Model were perhaps the most impressive and comprehensive. These methods are certainly the most holistic and all-encompassing from *top to bottom of the organization*, and *across all possible types of projects*. They begin with the strategic goals of the business and end with a list of projects to be undertaken. The process thus scores top marks for trying to link *projects undertaken* (i.e., where the money is spent) to *the goals* of the business.

This comprehensiveness, however, may also be the Achilles heel of the process. This is a huge model and framework to implement and use. It is sophisticated and somewhat difficult to fully comprehend; it requires much data, and it has many steps, each requiring hard work (especially from the senior management of the business). Whether management will stay the course here is an issue. By contrast, scoring model approaches – which build in strategic criteria and were described earlier in this chapter – are much simpler and less ambitious in scope. Implementation is rather straightforward by comparison.

When one strips away the complexities of the Strategic Buckets Model, the model really boils down to two major elements:

▶ a strategic exercise whereby desired spending levels are established for each project type (the "buckets" or target levels of spending); and,

▶ a rank ordering of projects within each bucket, using one of the traditional maximization methods (for example, via a scoring model; or a financial criterion such as NPV or ECV – see Chapter 2).

In this light, the model isn't quite as complex as it first appears.

One positive facet of the Strategic Buckets Model is the recognition that *all development projects which compete for the same resources can be considered in the portfolio approach.* Conceptually, this is quite correct. For example, product development projects must be considered along with cost reduction projects, because both utilize R&D resources.

A second feature is that different criteria can be used for different types of projects; therefore one is not faced with comparing and ranking very different types of projects against each other, an apples versus oranges situation. Because this is a two step approach (first allocate money to buckets, then prioritize like projects within a bucket), it is not necessary to arrive at a universal list of scoring or ranking criteria that fits all projects. Similar types of projects are only compared against each other. So, one is comparing all apples against each other within one bucket, and all oranges against each other in another bucket.

One company, which divided resources according to strategic buckets, used somewhat different criteria for trying to rank order projects within buckets. For example, for the bucket "Product Developments", one set of scoring model criteria was used – criteria that emphasized strategic fit, market attractiveness, and competitive advantage. For other buckets – namely cost reductions and process improvements – the ranking criteria changed to cost/ benefit and financial ones[*].

In this way the company was able to handle all projects competing for the same resources yet recognize the differences between projects, and recognize that selection criteria for different types of projects ought to be different.

Strategic Check[**]

This method is similar, in that it begins with the business's strategy and develops a strategic mission for each business. But it tends to be more of an "after-the-fact" model – a check or correction method designed to bring the portfolio back closer to the strategic ideal. Thus, instead of deliberately setting up buckets of resources, as in the Strategic Buckets Model above, this method simply begins with a complete portfolio ranking of all projects. For example, it might use a traditional maximization method (scoring model or financial criteria – see Chapter 2); and then checks that the resulting list of projects indeed is consistent with the business's strategy. The method is similar to the Strategic Buckets Model, except that it reverses the order of steps.

The strategic planning exercise used at the Royal Bank of Canada is fairly typical. Recall that Royal Bank uses a scoring model to rate and rank projects (refer to Exhibits 2.7 and 2.8). The "StratPlan" exercise is one check that the firm has built into its scoring technique to ensure that project spending is linked to strategy.

StratPlan is a *strategic planning exercise* whereby the 12 Product Groups in RBC are analyzed via a high level portfolio exercise. This StratPlan exercise results in missions and macro-strategies for each of the Product Groups. The *macro strategic exercise* is a fairly traditional one, but worth mentioning here because of the way it is tied to new product spending and the Royal Bank's scoring model. The process is this:

▶   First, the 12 Product Groups are scored on each of 18 rating scales (0-10 ratings) which capture three main factors: Market Attractiveness, Business Position, and Strategic Importance. The evaluators are from the Product

---

[*]   The argument here was that the characteristics of a successful new product are somewhat different than those for a successful process improvement, hence different selection criteria ought to be used. Further, since cost reductions or process improvements are internal projects, usually the financial outlook (or cost/benefit) is much more predictable, hence it ought to be a principal selection criterion for such projects. By contrast, for new products, the financial outlook is very often a highly uncertain estimate.

[**]   Another interesting approach for linking strategy to new product development has been developed by Product Development Partners, Inc. and incorporates a seven step model (see reference Chapter 4, No. 2).

Groups as well as other units and functions (Operations, Sales, Systems, etc.). Scoring takes place in an electronic meeting room, using a computer-based scoring technique along with a large screen computer display of results. Several rounds of scoring are necessary in order to arrive at consensus. The computer display highlights areas of inconsistencies and uncertainties requiring further discussion. Animated exchanges are usually part of this meeting. Note that evaluators from other units and functions – outside the business – keep the discussion "honest".

- ► Three portfolio maps or bubble diagrams are constructed from the scores, showing the locations of the 12 Product Groups on all three factors: Market Attractiveness, Business Position, and Strategic Importance.

- ► Based on their respective locations, each of the 12 Product Groups is then classed as a Diamond, Strong Box (cash generator), Wildcat or Cross-Roads business. A mission and vision are developed contingent on this classification, along with a strategy for each Product Group. Virtually all Groups are either Diamonds (which means a "growth" mission) or Strong Boxes (which translates into a "hold and maintain the course" mission and strategy). A few newer and smaller ones are Wildcats. Rarely is a product line classed as a Cross-Roads - these businesses have either been weeded out or merged with a unit in another part of the corporation.

So far, the exercise resembles a fairly standard strategic or SBU planning portfolio exercise, except perhaps for the use of electronic scoring. It is *the use of the classifications* – Diamond versus Strong Box versus Wildcat – as an input to the new product portfolio exercise that is the noteworthy part. Recall that the Royal Bank uses a scoring model which yields a single prioritized list of projects from all 12 Product Groups (see Exhibit 2.8). But this list *is only the first cut*. The list of projects "above the line" (i.e., judged as a Go) is quickly broken down by Product Group, and the total expenditures by Group are determined. Exhibit 4.4 portrays this process, adapted from the Royal Bank method. These totals, as a percentage of revenue, are then compared across Groups for inconsistencies. For example, the normal rule is that Diamond Product Groups should receive far more than their "fair share" of project spending – as much as double the norm. Conversely Strong Box Product Groups receive proportionately less. Gaps are identified among spending levels per business, based on the first cut list, versus the desired spending.

A second round of project prioritization ensues, with some projects originally "above the cut-off line" now being removed, while those below the line move up. This usually moves the project portfolio closer to the one dictated by the StratPlan exercise. Several rounds are required before the final list of projects "above the line" are agreed to. At this point, the prioritized list contains very good projects, according to the scoring model, and the spending allocations correctly reflect the various strategies and missions of each Product Group.

Exhibit 4.4: Royal Bank of Canada – Prioritized List of Projects by Product Group

RBC's First Cut Prioritized List of Projects					
Rank Order	Project Name	Product Group	Score (%)	Development Cost (S&T dollars $000)	Cumulative Development Cost ($000)
1	RBCash	Cash Management	83	2,400	2,400
2.	CashCore	Cash Management	76	1,920	4,320
3.	EBX	EDI	76	1,800	6,120
4.	EBY	EDI	73	500	6,620
5.	BuyAct	Deposits	73	6,000	12,620
6.	CorpPay	Payroll	70	2,000	14,620
7.	Project A- PC	Loans	70	1,600	16,220
8.	PC-MD	Loans	68	7,500	23,720
-	-	-	-	-	-
26	**Tiered/Interest Accounts**	**Deposits**	**55**	**930**	**90,150**
27	Tiered	Loans	52	1,000	
28	Trade-AP	Trade	52	1,200	
29	ATM-Y	Deposits	50	500	
.	.	.	.	.	.

Total Expenditure by Product Group

Target	Actual	Product Group
10%	18%	Cash Management
25%	30%	Deposits
5%	4%	Payroll
25%	15%	Loans
20%	13%	Disbursements
10%	11%	EDI
.	.	etc.

This StratPlan resembles the Strategic Buckets Model in that desired spending levels per area (in this case, by Product Group) are decided, gaps identified, and the portfolio of projects arranged accordingly. This method reverses the order of steps (projects are prioritized first, and then subsequently checked for consistency with strategy), is somewhat easier to implement, and is less demanding on management.

One SBU in Exxon Chemicals also uses a similar but after-the-fact strategic check. Here, all projects are prioritized using a scoring model, both at gate decision points and during periodic portfolio review meetings. The split in annual spending is then displayed in a newness matrix (Exhibit 4.1). Imbalances become evident, and spending adjustments are made for the up-coming year.

Summary

This chapter concludes our discussion on the three portfolio management goals – maximization of value, balance and strategic alignment. In the next chapter, we begin to look at the actual design and implementation of a Portfolio Management Process for your company. Chapter 5 starts by identifying the various problems and pitfalls that other companies have experienced. This, in turn, will permit you to preempt much of the learning curve that other organizations have had to undergo the hard way. Chapters 6 and 7 outline how to design a Portfolio Management Process tailored to the needs of your own organization.

Chapter 5

Problems, Pitfalls and Unresolved Issues

Thirty years of development of portfolio schemes, and are we any further ahead? The answer is clearly yes! At worst, we've discovered *what does not work* in portfolio management. More positively, some companies are very close to a solution that works for them. But there remain many unresolved issues and barriers yet to be overcome. This chapter highlights our major conclusions, identifies the problem areas and leads up to our recommendations in the final two chapters.

General Conclusions

Portfolio Management is a Vital Issue

The portfolio management question is a *very important one* – perhaps more important than we had previously judged. If the amount of time and money that firms are spending on the problem is any indication, then portfolio management and project selection is likely the *number one issue in new product development* and technology management for the next decade. It may even be in the top three or four strategic issues faced by today's corporations.

Portfolio management is critical for at least three reasons, according to companies we interviewed:

1. First, a successful new product effort is *fundamental to corporate success* as we move into the next century. More so than ever, senior management recognizes the need for new products, especially the right new products. This logically translates into portfolio management: the ability to select today projects that will become tomorrow's new product winners.

2. Second, new product development is the *manifestation of the business's strategy*. That is, one important way a company operationalizes strategy is through the new products that it develops. If its new product initiatives are wrong, then the company fails at implementing its business strategy. The new product choices one makes today define the business tomorrow.

3. Third, portfolio management is about *resource allocation*. In a business world preoccupied with value to the shareholder and doing more with less, technology and marketing resources are simply too scarce to allocate to the wrong projects. The consequences of poor portfolio management are evident: the firm squanders scarce resources on the wrong projects. As a result, the truly meritorious projects are starved.

No Magic Solution

There is no magic answer or *black box model* to solve the portfolio management challenge. Indeed the firms we studied – in spite of expensive and extensive attempts to develop such portfolio models – were quick to admit that there was no single "right" answer here. They said they were still actively seeking solutions and making improvements to their own approaches.

Not only is there no magic answer, there is not even a *dominant approach*! In spite of the fact that many of these executives had read the same reports, articles and books, had benchmarked against the same firms, and had even hired many of the same consultants, the approaches they arrived at for their own companies were quite different from each other. There is no universal method, dominant theme or generic model here; rather, the models and approaches employed were quite firm specific.

A great variety of concepts, tools and approaches were employed by these leading firms. The most popular were sophisticated variants on *scoring models* and *financial indices*, and also various *portfolio mapping* approaches, such as bubble diagrams. Some progressive firms used a hybrid approach: a combination that looked at the issues of *balancing the portfolio* as well as *maximizing the value of the portfolio against certain objectives*.

There was no evidence at all of use of, or interest in, mathematical programming and optimization techniques. Ironically, such models were very common in the literature, but had rarely been implemented or tested in industry. Indeed, the notion of a "black box decision model" that would yield a prioritized list of projects had been rejected by all firms studied. Instead, a *decision tool* or *decision support system* designed to help managers make the decision was preferred.

No "Flavor of the Month" Solutions

The problem is far from solved. Many of the models we observed in companies, although elegant and comprehensive, were as yet relatively untested. These are largely new approaches being implemented only now in these firms. No doubt there will be years of work before well-accepted portfolio models and schemes are common place in industry.

In spite of the lack of quick and easy solutions, virtually all of the firms in our study had arrived at moderately satisfactory approaches. No solution was easy to come by, however. Developing a portfolio approach proved much more difficult, time-consuming and expensive than initially expected*. Nonetheless, the progress made by some companies is encouraging. In the final two chapters, we offer a glimpse into the solutions to managing the portfolio of projects. These insights are based on the varied experiences of firms in our study.

---

* We estimate two of the firms that we investigated in depth had probably spent close to $500,000 each on outside consultants to resolve the portfolio management problem. Two other firms had likely spent almost this amount in staff time and consultants combined.

But first, let's have a closer look at the problems and issues that were encountered by our sample of companies – problems that we hope to resolve in Chapters 6 and 7.

Specific Conclusions Regarding Effective Portfolio Management

Our investigation revealed 14 key issues that managers must address in developing portfolio management approaches. They are summarized in Exhibit 5.1 and explained in more detail below.

Exhibit 5.1:   Challenges in Designing an Effective Portfolio Management Process

1. What is the main goal of your portfolio management model?
2. Does the model allow you to maximize the value of the portfolio against some objective(s)?
3. Does the model permit you to seek the right balance of projects?
4. Is the model very closely tied to your business's strategy?
5. How will the integration between gate decisions and portfolio decisions be handled?
6. Is the model consistent with the quality of information available?
7. How firm are resource commitments, once a project is designated a "Go" in the portfolio?
8. How will you handle projects that are put on hold?
9. Is it necessary to have prioritized or rank ordered lists of projects at all?
10. What types of projects will be considered in the portfolio model? Do you compare all projects competing for resources against all others or only compare similar types of projects?
11. What is the right role for the portfolio model: to facilitate and/or display information for managers? Or to be a decision model?
12. How do you avoid information overload?
13. How do you gather and present the required information and data needed?
14. How do you deal with the problems that the financial analysis creates (e.g. unreliable forecasts, implied accuracy, cannibalization, terminal values)?

1. Three Main Goals

Three goals provided the underpinnings of portfolio approaches. These were:

- <u>Maximizing the value of the portfolio</u> against objectives, such as profitability or strategic importance. Here financially-based methods (such as ECV) and scoring models (which built the desired objectives into the criteria) were most effective.

- <u>Balance in the portfolio</u>: Portfolios can be balanced in terms of numerous dimensions. The most popular were risk versus reward; ease versus attractiveness; and breakdown by project type, market and product line. Visual models, especially bubble diagrams, were thought to be most appropriate to portray balance.

- <u>Link to strategy</u>: Strategic alignment – strategic fit and resource allocation reflecting the business's strategy – were the issues here. Scoring models, strategic buckets, and strategic checks were the appropriate techniques.

Of the three, no one goal seemed to dominate; moreover, no one portfolio model or approach seemed capable of delivering all three goals.

2. Maximizing the Value of the Portfolio Against Some Objective

Maximizing value is an obvious goal for portfolio management. Yet some of the techniques, notably the visual maps, were not particularly effective here. For example, mapping techniques did not logically lead to the "best" portfolio of projects.

The maximization goal was made more challenging when multiple objectives, such as NPV, IRR and strategic importance, were sought concurrently. The four methods that worked best in these respects included:

- The ECV, a financial model based on a decision tree, as practiced at English China Clay, incorporates probabilities and recognizes that some costs are not incurred if the project is aborted.

- The productivity index, a financial index, considers the ratio of payoffs (risk adjusted NPV) to the R&D expenditures.

- The dynamic rank ordered list, as found at Company G, is again largely financial and has the advantage of considering several objectives concurrently, including non-financial criteria.

- The scoring model, which was the least financial of the three, and captured multiple objectives and/or desired characteristics of projects, was used by both Hoechst and The Royal Bank. The former had developed an excellent list of scoring criteria; the latter used a novel method of obtaining scoring data from senior management.

3. Seeking Portfolio Balance

Maximizing the value against an objective is *not the only decision rule* in selecting a portfolio of projects. There is also a need to achieve the right balance of projects on a number of different dimensions. For example companies should look for the right mix of long term versus short term projects; or high risk versus low risk; or offensive versus defensive; or step-out versus close-to-home products, and so on. For these dimensions, *more is not necessarily better*; rather, the goal is to achieve the *right mix or balance*. Scoring models are clearly inappropriate here, as they tend to rank projects in terms of maximization against an objective – the more, the better. Thus, various mapping approaches are more useful, such as, bubble diagram risk-versus-reward maps, or pie charts and histograms, which portray the split in resources by timing or across project types, markets, and product lines. In particular, bubble diagrams or portfolio maps provide a visual portrayal of the portfolio, where balance or distribution of projects can be seen and debated.

Some visual maps also have the advantage of being able to hint at the appropriate portfolio. For example, in the risk-reward maps, certain quadrants denote projects that are clearly better than others. One quadrant contains "white elephant" projects, suggesting that pruning is needed. Thus, although mapping and chart models are information display methods and effectively portray balance, they are also one important input to the maximization of the portfolio's value.

4. Link to Strategy

Portfolio management – that is, the selection and prioritization of specific R&D projects – must be *very closely tied to strategic decisions*. Strategic alignment has two meanings, with subtle but important differences:

- First, portfolio management must ensure *strategic fit* – that all projects are "on strategy" and consistent with the direction of the corporation. For example, senior management defines the arenas of focus – the product, market and technology areas on which to focus – and then selects projects only within these boundaries.

- Second, and most important, portfolio management must *allocate spending* across projects so as to *mirror the strategy* of the business. For example, if the business's strategy is very much a growth one, then the majority of spending on new product projects should be on business and market development projects, rather than on merely "maintain the business" projects.

Traditional portfolio models, such as mathematical programming models, have failed to account for this strategic link. The three best examples we witnessed in which the portfolio-strategy link was well handled included:

- The Strategic Buckets Model: This is an elaborate scheme which begins with the business unit's strategy and culminates in the designation of envelopes, or buckets, of money for different types of projects. Within these buckets, projects are ranked ordered and prioritized. In this way, the spending allocation mirrors the strategic direction and desired spending patterns of the business.

- Scoring models: These are comprised of multiple scoring scales, some of which capture strategic direction, as illustrated by the Hoechst method. By using a large number of scoring criteria that rate projects in terms of strategic fit, strategic impact and strategic leverage, this company ensures that the right projects – from a strategic perspective – rise to the top of the pile.

- Strategic Check: The Royal Bank's StratPlan exercise classes business units and defines strategic missions for each, which then become major inputs to the allocation of resources in the portfolio selection exercise (Exhibit 4.3). At Exxon Chemical, some SBUs check for spending breakdowns after-the-fact (Exhibit 4.1) which leads to adjustments for the up-coming year.

5. Integration Between Gate Decisions and Portfolio Decisions

All the companies we studied relied on some type of new product process model, such as Stage-Gate, to drive new product projects from idea through to market. Embedded within these processes are gates or Go/Kill decisions points. The gates are, in effect, resource allocation decisions, where the senior decision-makers or "gatekeepers" make Go/Kill and prioritization decisions on individual projects.

A potential for conflict exists between this gating decision process and portfolio management, namely:

- real time decisions are made on individual projects at gates; versus
- portfolio decisions are made periodically, but on all projects together.

These are two different decision processes (and in some firms, even involve different people and somewhat different criteria!); yet both purport to select projects and allocate resources, hence the potential for conflict. For example:

- Portfolio decisions consider all projects together - a comparison of one against another. This holistic view is healthy, but it does limit the amount of time the decision-makers can spend on any one project. By contrast, gate decisions tend to focus on only one project: that one project receives a thorough management review, but in relative isolation from the other projects.

- Gate decisions occur in real time as the project moves from one stage to the next. By contrast, portfolio decision meetings are held in calender time, perhaps annually, semi-annually, or quarterly.

Given these two decision processes, the questions become: Which process should dominate? How should the two processes be integrated?

Some firms, particularly those whose portfolio schemes have been in place for some time, have developed rules or conflict resolution methods. These rules tend to let one or the other decision scheme dominate, for example:

- *The portfolio model* dominates: The Royal Bank has developed a set of decision rules to integrate the portfolio model with gate decisions. Here, the annual portfolio meeting ear-marks funds for certain projects for the next year (there are quarterly updates, so the portfolio list is relatively current). But merely being "in the portfolio" does not guarantee funding or Go decisions. Each project still has to pass each gate. In short, the gate decisions can override the portfolio decisions. In practice, however, it is rare that a project, once approved at a portfolio meeting, is rejected at a gate meeting (unless the project is in serious trouble). In effect, the portfolio meeting takes precedence.

- *The gates dominate:* Hoechst management is adamant that the gate decisions take precedence. Here, the portfolio review is viewed only as a *course correction*. The view is: "Make sound decisions at the gates and the portfolio will take care of itself." The argument is that one might not achieve the optimal balance or mix of projects, but if the gates have been rigorous, at least all the projects in the portfolio will be good ones.

We conclude that both decision approaches – gate decisions and portfolio reviews – have their merits:

- As noted above, decisions made at gates are focused on single projects. Gate reviews can last hours, they are in-depth, they utilize many criteria, and they have access to current information. Thus, the decision is likely to be a more thoughtful one for that particular project. But the decision is made in relative isolation (all projects are not considered together); and the project may not be prioritized against either all other active or on-hold projects.

- Portfolio reviews are holistic; they consider all projects together and may even take into account the ideal balance of projects as well as the desire to maximize against an objective. But with all projects considered in one meeting, the discussion on any one project is likely to be limited and superficial. Moreover, the data may not be the most current. For example, the data used to develop portfolio maps or lists is often retrieved from a databank whose input comes from the most recent gate meeting for each project, which may have been months ago for some projects.

Neither decision approach is robust enough to eliminate the need for the other; thus, both methods must be married to yield the best portfolio and project selection decisions.

Reckitt & Colman has developed an useful scheme to link gate decisions with their portfolio model. Recall that Reckitt & Colman's portfolio model features a number of maps: Ease versus Attractiveness; Probability of Success versus NPV; and so on. Before projects are considered in the portfolio analysis, the project must first pass the Gate 3 criteria. (This is the gate before major development funds are spent.) If the project passes the Gate 3 hurdles or Must criteria, then the project is subjected to a project selection model. Here criteria are considered in a scoring model format. The project scores are compared with standard hurdles preset for the product category. Thus, individual new projects are not compared to the whole portfolio, but to hurdle scores that ensure the minimum standards of the portfolio are met. These hurdles are adjusted periodically to favor certain types of projects desired in the portfolio. Exhibit 5.2 provides a flow chart to illustrate the decision process.

Quite separately, portfolio reviews are conducted periodically; they review the balance and mix of active projects, and set the minimum hurdles for the gate scoring model accordingly (i.e., to correct portfolio imbalances).

Exhibit 5.2: Reckitt & Colman's Logic Flowchart of Selection Model

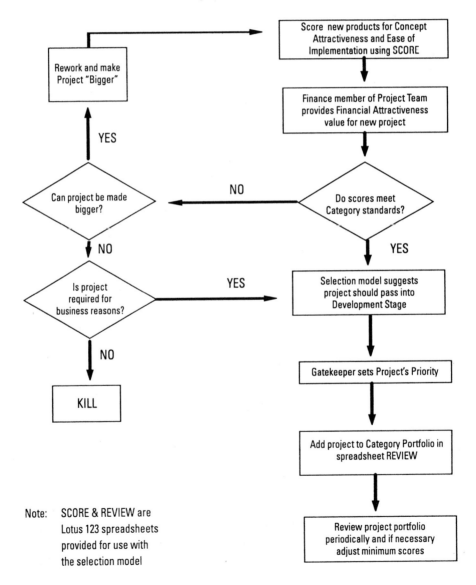

Note: SCORE & REVIEW are Lotus 123 spreadsheets provided for use with the selection model

6. Imaginary Precision

While useful, portfolio models should not be over-used, nor their results necessarily believed. Recall the criticism that using a scoring model imputed a degree of precision that simply did not exist: "They're trying to measure a [soft] banana with a micrometer!". The same concern was voiced for other models as well.

A universal weakness was that virtually every model we studied implied a degree of precision far beyond people's ability to provide reliable date. That is, the model's sophistication far exceeded the quality of the data. Ironically, some managements confessed to being mesmerized by their models into believing that the data was accurate. The financial models, rank ordered lists or bubble diagrams appear so elegant that one sometimes forgets how imprecise the data is upon which these diagrams or charts are constructed.

Clearly, before one proceeds to develop even more sophisticated portfolio approaches, there is a great need to bring the quality of the data up to the levels required by the current models. Three key areas have been identified where data is consistently weak:

- Poor market information, including estimates of market size, expected revenue and pricing plagues many projects. Not only is inadequate market analysis and poor market research cited as the number one reason for new product failure, but is also a major cause of difficulties in portfolio management and project selection.

- Technical success estimates (probabilities of technical success) have proven elusive for many managers, especially in the pre-development stages. Various consensus, Delphi or decision tree techniques have been employed, but the fact remains that predicting the probability of technical success remain problematic for some types of projects.

- Manufacturing and capital cost estimates are also difficult to obtain, especially during the earlier phases of a project. Note that many firms require a financial analysis prior to the beginning of development, and these financial data (such as NPV) become inputs to the portfolio model. The problem is that the product is not even developed yet. Still, manufacturing (including material) costs and capital equipment needs are estimated.

7. Shifting Resource Commitments

Should viable and active projects be killed, just because a better one comes along? We encountered very different philosophies here:

> View No. 1: Resource commitments to projects *are not firm*. Resources should be moved at will from one active project to another project. For example, even though one project has been given a Go and resources have been committed, and even if it remains a positive one, when a better project comes along, resources can be stripped from the first project to feed the second (for example Rhode &

Schwarz's[*] new portfolio approach uses an adaptation of this method). The argument here is that management must have the flexibility to optimally allocate resources, regardless of commitments previously made to project teams.

One implication is that the portfolio is a *very dynamic one*, constantly changing (no project has a firm Go commitment); and the portfolio of projects must constantly be reviewed. A dynamic portfolio management method is essential here.

View No. 2: Resource commitments *are quite firm*. That is, resource commitments made to project teams must be kept – for the sake of continuity and team morale – even if a more attractive project comes along. The notion here is that while it may be desirable to have resource flexibility in order to allocate resources optimally, team morale and the negative implications of "jerking around" project teams and leaders are more important. Further, if projects are "on again, off agin", there is a great waste of resources and time. Shifting resources from one project to the next is not seamless. Start-ups and shut-downs cost time and money. Finally, newer projects always look better than ones that are partway through development (warts always seem to appear as time passes!), so that the inevitable outcome is that resources are stripped from projects

Exhibit 5.3:
Red Flags for Projects

New product projects sometimes encounter problems. Often original estimates are revised that render the project less attractive. When a flag situation occurs, the project leader must inform gatekeepers immediately, who may call for an immediate gate review. Here are some red flags:

Project Schedule: if the project falls behind schedule by more than 30 days, according to the agreed-to timeline.

Project Budget: if the project goes over budget by more than 5% at a point (e.g., versus milestone projections), defined in the plan approved at the previous gate.

Resources: if any major functional area is unable to meet on-going resource commitments according to the agreed to timeline.

Product Cost: if any change in the expected product cost occurs (e.g., manufacturing cost) that is greater than 5% above cost estimates provided at the last gate.

Sales Forecast: if any change greater than 10% occurs in the number of forecast sales units; or if any change occurs in the configuration ratios (product mix) that impacts margin by more than 3%.

Business Case: if any change occurs that impacts significantly on the business case and financial outlook for the project (more than 5% impact).

Product Specs: whenever the product design or product requirements are revised and impact negatively on meeting a customer need or the product specs.

Service: whenever a change in the service and support planned for the product occurs, which impacts negatively on a customer need or requirement.

Quality: if product quality metrics fall outside 0.3 sigma value.

---

[*]   Rhode & Schwarz is an electronics company located in Germany.

in their later phases to support new ones. Taken to an extreme, no project ever is completed!

One implication of this second philosophy is that the portfolio of projects has some stability. As a consequence, the portfolio of projects does not need to be reviewed quite so frequently, nor does the portfolio management scheme need to be quite so dynamic.

Generally companies with a longer term perspective and considerable experience in major new product projects embraced the more stable view that resource commitments are firm (for example, some of the chemical companies we interviewed). Firms in shorter term projects and in very dynamic markets leaned more towards the flexible resource model (for example, some of the non-durable consumer goods firms in the study).

Even among companies that embraced the "committed resources" view (No. 2), there were differences regarding just *how long or firm the commitment was*. All agreed that if the project "shot itself" – that is, ran into serious problems with such things as delays, negative changes in the business case or technical barriers – the project must be reviewed immediately. This review or immediate gate meeting could change the resource commitment and even kill the project. Some companies had even developed lists of red flags that signalled problems and required the project leader to call for an immediate project review. Exhibit 5.3 provides a sample list of red flags from one firm.

Assuming the project avoided red flags and remained in good shape – met milestones, continued to look financially attractive, and so on – then how firm is the commitment?

At Exxon Chemical, the commitment is firm until the next gate. That is, "Once resources are committed, they are not expected to be changed until the next Gate review, barring an extraordinary development in the project.".[1] In short, at each gate in Exxon's process, the project "is up for grabs". The implication here is that the project can be re-prioritized at each gate. The portfolio model is applied at each gate decision point, and the portfolio of projects – including where this one projects fits in – is discussed at each gate meeting.

At other firms, the commitment is made *right through to the end of the project*. That is, barring negative results or red flags, commitments made at the "Go to Development" decision point are firm through to launch. The project still has to pass all gates and reviews, and could still be killed in the event of negative information.

The implication of this commitment model is that really there is *only one major decision point* in the new product process, and as long as the project remains in good shape, it continues to obtain needed resources. Thus, the role of gates is to provide a critical review to ensure the project remains sound. The portfolio model applies to *one key decision point only*, where the proposed project is compared to all on-going active projects and to those in the queue (on Hold).

8. Too Many Projects "On Hold"

More projects pass the gate criteria than there are resources to fund them. This places even greater pressure on the prioritization process. In some firms interviewed, the list of projects "on hold" was far longer than the list of active projects!

The problem here is that no one – especially senior managers – wants to kill potentially good projects, even when it is recognized that:

- there are likely a number of other projects better than this one; and,
- prioritization decisions are essential to achieving focus – this means killing projects.

So it becomes much more convenient to start a "Hold Tank", and dump good projects into this tank. The implicit argument is this: A kill decision is averted and no one's feelings are hurt. Besides, someday there may be resources available to do some of the projects in the "Hold Tank" (often wishful thinking on the part of the senior gatekeepers).

When it first implemented its stage-gate new product process, ECC encountered this hold problem. Quickly, a log-jam of projects awaiting entry to development occurred. By the time the hold list exceeded the active project list by a factor of two, managers knew they were in difficulty. A new decision rule was instituted: a project can remain on hold for no longer than three months. After that, it's "up or out" - either it becomes an active and resourced project, or it's killed. A tough rule perhaps, but at least it forces the gate decision makers (gatekeepers) to be more discriminating, and to really make the needed decisions. Further, it has forced gatekeepers to search for additional funding and resources for meritorious projects that are in danger of being killed.

9. Why Have a Prioritized or Rank-Ordered List at All?

This is a philosophical question: According to management in one leading firm, there are only three classes of projects:

- funded and active projects with people assigned;
- good projects with no one working on them (currently unfunded) - these are the Hold projects; and,
- dead projects.

If there are only three types, why the need for rank-ordered lists? In this instance, management believed there was no great need for a prioritization or scoring scheme (as outlined in Chapter 2), or any other model which led to a rank ordered list. All that was needed was a *triage approach*: active, hold or dead!

A contrary opinion expressed at many other firms is that a rank ordered list is not only important, it is necessary. For example, even though a project is "Go", there are *varying degrees of "Go"*, depending on the project's importance, pay-offs, and priority. As an illustration, management at Hoechst regularly selects a sub-set of active projects and performs a *full court press* on these; that is, they resource these chosen projects to the maximum, ensuring that they are done as quickly as possible. Given that different levels of resource commitments can be made to any project, logic dictates that not only must projects be separated into "Go" and "Hold" categories, but that "Go" projects themselves must be prioritized. Those top priority projects receive maximum resources for a timely completion.

10. Must Consider all Projects

There is a view that all projects that compete for the same resources ought to be considered in the portfolio approach. This includes new product projects as well as process improvements, cost reductions, fundamental research, and so on. Conceptually this is quite correct, but it does increase the magnitude of the portfolio problem. Rather than simply comparing one new product project to another, now management must deal with a myriad of different types of projects, a much more complex decision situation.

This issue of whether all projects should be compared against each other yields proponents on both sides of the argument. Some firms studied simply set aside envelopes of money for different types of projects. Within each envelope, projects are rated and ranked against each other. The Strategic Buckets Model outlined in Chapter 4 is an example of this route. This approach solves two thorny problems:

- First, the Strategic Buckets Model removes the task of comparing and ranking unlike projects against each other. Ranking dissimilar projects against each other is a very difficult task for these reasons:
  - ► The nature and quality of information differs greatly between project types. For example, a process improvement project is likely to have fairly certain cost and benefit estimates, while a new product project does not, especially early in the project.
  - ► The criteria for comparison are likely different. The most important criterion for a cost reduction project may be cost-benefit; for a new product project, it may be strategic importance and sustainable competitive advantage.

  So how does one compare two projects when even the criteria for a good project differ? Via the Strategic Buckets Model, the task is simplified: one uses different scoring schemes and quite different criteria for rating projects in different buckets.

- Second, by setting aside buckets of money or resources, one is assured that spending and resource allocation mirrors the business's strategy. Recall that this is the major strength of the Strategic Buckets Model: It forces resources to be allocated into buckets a priori.

The opposing viewpoint is that all projects should compete against each other and that there should be no pool of money or resources set aside for any particular type of project. For example, if all the product development projects are superior to all the process improvement projects, then all the resources ought to go to the product development projects – survival of the fittest. In short, the merits of each project should decide the total split of resources, rather than having some artificial and a priori split in resources.

11. Information Display Versus a Decision Scheme

Should the portfolio scheme merely *display information to managers* in a useful way (as bubble diagrams do); or should it produce a *prioritized list of projects* (as a scoring model or dynamic ranked ordered list does)? The *display approach* means that management must review the various maps and charts, integrate the information, and then arrive at prioritized lists themselves. By contrast, the *prioritized list* approach provides management with a "first cut" list of projects, prioritized according to certain criteria: Management then reviews and adjusts the list as needed.

Managers interviewed were divided on this issue:

- A common view was that the portfolio model ought to be an input to the portfolio meeting, discussion and decision. But the ranking of projects into a final prioritized list must be very much a non-mechanistic process. There are simply too many factors, many of them "soft" that are far beyond the capability of any decision-making scheme to capture. Managers are the decision-makers, not a decision model.

- An opposite view was that mangers are not necessarily makers of consistent and good decisions. If a model can be developed that captures most of the considerations that should enter the portfolio decision, then at least part of the managerial decision process can be replaced by this model. Moreover, these models, such as a financially-based ranked list or a scoring model, only provide a first cut at the list of projects: Management retains the final say on the exact prioritization. They adjust the list to capture factors not considered by the portfolio model.

12. Information Overload

One deficiency with certain mapping approaches is the large number of possible maps. Admittedly, portfolio selection is a complex problem, and one is tempted to plot everything against everything. As noted in Chapter 3, there are many possible parameters to consider. Indeed the possible permutations of X-Y plots, histograms and pie charts are almost endless.

Are managers simply overwhelmed with all the information and plots? Experience in some firms suggests they are. For example, when first conceived, Reckitt & Colman's portfolio approach contained far more maps and charts than the final version now in use. Managers quickly realized that they needed to simplify the problem and boil the decision down to a few key parameters and a few important charts. In Chapter 3, we illustrated some of the more useful maps and charts from among the many we saw in companies:

- the Reward versus Probability-of-Success bubble diagram.
- the Concept Attractiveness versus Ease-of-Implementation bubble diagram.
- the timing histogram (where resources are being spent and projects by year of launch).
- various pie chart breakdowns: project types, markets and product lines.

13. Acquiring the Needed Information on Projects

Often portfolio management must deal with dozens of projects, both new and existing. One problem is acquiring and presenting the data (or profile information) on these many projects.

> In one health care products company, project leaders claimed they were being "driven to distraction" by the amount and detail of information required by the portfolio manager and the consulting firm he had hired. Very detailed financial information, uncertainty estimates, and resource requirement data were required for each and every project – data far beyond that normally required for regular gate meetings. Project leaders complained bitterly about how much time this "make work" task was taking, when often their projects were suffering from lack of time and attention. Others had simply given up, and had resorted to providing nonsense data.

Portfolio models invariably require at least some data on all the projects in the pipeline. This means that a pipeline database must be established. It also means that methods for routinely collecting and inputting the vital data must be established.

> When Company T first implemented the bubble diagram approach to portfolio management, the data collection task was thought to be a relatively easy one to the portfolio model manager. "Data on NPV, likelihoods of success, resources being spent, and a few other pieces of information for every project seemed like a straightforward information request I made of each project leader," he explained. But it took more than three months to gather this "readily available" data, often after considerable arm-twisting.

One possible solution is that only existing projects that have passed at least some gate reviews – for example, the Go to Development decision point – should be considered in the portfolio scheme. This greatly reduces the number of projects under consideration, with a corresponding decrease in the amount of data required. This approach also means that the results of the "Go to Development" gate review – for example, financial data, resource requirements, and probabilities – can be collected right at the gate meeting and be used as input data to the portfolio model.

14. Financial Analysis Methods Pose Problems

For most firms, strict reliance on financial methods and criteria in order to prioritize projects was considered inappropriate. Financial data are simply too unreliable during the course of a project, especially in the earlier phases when prioritization decisions are most needed. Post project reviews suggested that estimates on key variables, such as expected revenues and profits at the "Go to Development" decision point were highly inaccurate. Yet this is the point at which serious resource commitments are made and the project enters the portfolio scheme.

A second problem was that sophisticated financial models and spreadsheets often implied a level of reliability beyond the facts on which the data were based on. Computer spreadsheets in some firms had become quite complex, and produced best case and worst case scenarios, sensitivity analysis, and so on. Managers were often mesmerized by these in a gate or portfolio meeting. They began to believe the financial projections (due in part to the elegance of the financial model and the dazzling output it produced) and lost sight of the fact that the data inputs were highly unreliable.

Even when valid financial data were available and reasonably reliable, there were still problems. Here are some examples:

- How does one deal with the possible *cannibalization of other products* already in the product line? Often negative interrelationships among products – especially between new and existing ones – are complex. Hence quantitative estimates are difficult to arrive at. For example, a new product might be expected to cannibalize the sales of an old product in the company's lineup. But at how fast a rate? Reliable estimates are very difficult to make. And this argument was often heard: "If we don't cannibalize our own products, a competitor surely will; thus, no cannibalization costs effects should be borne by the new product." The issue is difficult to resolve.

- How one treats the *capital cost requirements* is another complex issue, especially in the case of *shared facilities* or *idle facilities*. For example, one capital intensive product developer always faced the problem of determining the cost of spare production capacity on capital equipment. How much of this cost should the new product project bear? Some pundits in the company argued "none". They reasoned that, after all, the equipment is idle and that there is no opportunity or incremental capital cost. Others in that company made a case that the new product should bear a "fair share" of the equipment capital costs, even when equipment was otherwise idle. Finally, the argument often was that the equipment may be idle this year, but may not be next year, so there really is an opportunity cost.

- How does one treat *terminal values* of projects? That is, what is the project "worth" at the end of the five or ten year projection considered in the cash flow analysis. An assumption that the project is worth nothing after, say, ten years could penalize a project severely, especially in the case of projects where the internal rate of return (IRR) is relatively low and close to the hurdle rate*.

The Royal Bank had developed a standardized, compiled spreadsheet analysis for use in all business cases from their "Go to Development" gate onward. This standard

---

*   Note that when the IRR (or discount rate) is quite high in a 10-year cash flow analysis, the value of income earned in year 11 is almost negligible. For example, suppose we undertook a 10-year cash flow analysis of a project, which had profits of $1 million in year 10. One might logically argue that the project is still worth something in year 11, say, 10 times the earnings of the previous year. So we value the project at $10 million in year 11. If this is discounted at 15%, then this adds 2.1 million to the NPV of the project, which might make the difference between a Go and Kill decision. If discounted at 35%, however, this $10 million amounts to only $350,000, likely a negligible amount to the total value of the project.

10-year cash flow model provides three assumptions, or treatments, of the terminal value:

- ▸ the project has no terminal value in year 11;
- ▸ the project is worth 5 times of year 10 earnings in year 11; and
- ▸ the project is worth 10 times of year 10 earnings in year 11.

For each assumption, both the NPV and IRR are calculated. Management can then view the effects of the three different terminal value treatments, and judge accordingly. Interestingly, often the three different treatments yield quite different IRR or NPV results.

The Path Forward

Overcoming the challenge of developing an effective portfolio approach for your company is no small task. In today's business environment, there is no question that portfolio management is a vital issue. Our investigation points to several fundamental truths, however: Do not expect a "magic solution" here! And the "flavor of the month" solution probably will not work long term. We also found a number of issues that must be addressed by management in order to develop an effective Portfolio Management Process (summarized in Exhibit 5.1). Our fourteen conclusions naturally lead to the next question: Now that we know the different approaches and have identified a number of challenges, how do we do it? In the next two chapters we present our recommendations on how to develop a Portfolio Management Process for your company.

Chapter 6

Managing Your Portfolio

The Right Portfolio Scheme

Which portfolio management method is right for you? In Chapters 2-4, we examined the portfolio approaches used by leading firms: We had a glimpse into the strengths and weaknesses of these methods, and into some of the thorny issues faced. Now the money question: *Which approach is best?*

This is not an easy question, because there is no single best answer. In these final two chapters, we map out the preferred portfolio approaches, and we indicate which ones are most appropriate for different situations. Our recommendations are based, in part, on what managers told us worked and did not. They are also based on our own attempts to implement portfolio schemes within firms.

Let's now provide a road map for this chapter and the next. In this chapter, we:

- consider briefly the top level decision regarding *allocation of resources* across Business Units;
- provide a *strategy-process matrix* that helps in deciding which Portfolio Management Process (PMP) is right for your company and Business Unit;
- define what is meant by *business strategy and new product strategy;*
- provide an overview of the components of an appropriate Portfolio Management Process for each of four situations or quadrants in the strategy-process matrix.

And in the next chapter:

- For the best, yet most complex of these situations – where your business has both a well-defined new product strategy, and also an effective new product process or Stage-Gate system in place – we provide a detailed description of the components of a PMP.

The Portfolio Management Process is illustrated throughout these discussions via a real but disguised example of a business unit in a large corporation. We will call this business the Agro division.

Top Level Resource Allocation

Portfolio management for new products is about resource allocation; namely, how to allocate your scarce human and financial resources across various projects and potential projects. In medium and larger firms, we cannot escape the macro-allocation question: What about total resource allocation across Business Units (BUs)?

Resource allocation across BUs is a top level issue. It deals with corporate strategy and planning at the highest level and is certainly beyond the scope of this chapter. While methods vary by firm, Exhibit 6.1 provides a typical framework. Here, the corporation decides strategy and direction (top of Exhibit 6.1). Resources are then allocated to individual BUs (downward arrow in Exhibit 6.1). Concurrently, each BU develops its own business and new product strategy. In this way, opportunities and resource needs are identified and fed upward as input to the corporate strategy (upward arrow in Exhibit 6.1), which in turn impacts the resource allocations.

Exhibit 6.1: Corporate Strategy Linkage to Business Unit Strategy

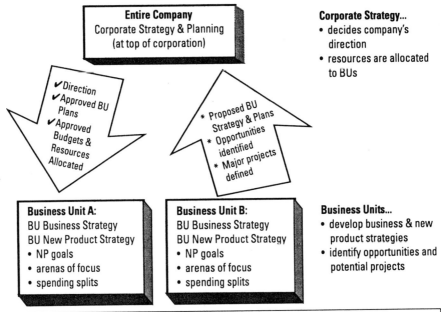

Sub-Optimizing at the BU Level

Should R&D resources be allocated to BUs, which then decide which projects to do? Or should all projects from all BUs be prioritized against each other – in a centralized fashion?

The argument against BUs managing their own portfolios is this: Suppose your corporation has three BUs; further, suppose each BU is given enough resources to do two major new product projects each. So six projects in total are selected. But what if Business Unit A's first six projects are better than the four projects selected by the other two BUs! Shouldn't Business Unit A's six projects be done (i.e., A receives <u>all</u> the money)? Not so, according to a decentralized scheme... each BU does its two projects, which is sub-optimization! The counter argument is that a solid corporate planning and resource allocation model – like the BCG or McKinsey/GE models described – will recognize that Business Unit A has much better opportunities, and allocate more money here in the first place... but that this allocation decision is a corporate planning, high level one.

A major reason for a decentralized project portfolio approach is that the BU senior management is much closer to the market and technology: thus they're in a better knowledge position to make the Go/Kill and prioritization decisions needed on projects ... certainly a far better position than a group of corporate executives at the top!

If your firm has deficiencies here, note that there have been many schemes proposed over the years for deciding resource allocations across BUs. Indeed, we saw evidence of some of these while undertaking our portfolio study. Perhaps the best known schemes for resource allocation across businesses are in the McKinsey/GE and BCG models.[1]

These models are corporate strategy and planning models. Essentially, each BU is scored or rated on various factors, which are then combined into several major dimensions. Depending on the model, the axes or main dimensions usually boil down to Market Attractiveness and Business Position. That is: is the BU facing an attractive market? And, is the BU a strong one – well poised to attack the market? A two-by-two or three-by-three cell matrix is constructed and BUs are located on this two dimensional matrix (see Exhibit 6.2).

Exhibit 6.2: Typical Corporate Allocation Model

Business Strength

		Strong	Medium	Weak
Market Attractiveness	High	**Stars**		**Problem Child or Wildcat**
	Medium			
	Low	**Cash Cow**		**Dog**

Business Units are classed into one of the 9 cells. A mission and strategy are decided; resources are allocated. Adaptation of the General Electric (GE) model.

Each BU develops a strategic mission, which depends in part on its location on the matrix. For example, the BCG model classifies BUs as cash cows, stars, dogs and problem children, and provides suggested strategies or a mission for each.

Resource allocation then ensues. The matrix location (which cell the BU is in according to Exhibit 6.2), together with the strategic mission for the BU, helps determine how much funding the unit receives. Both R&D monies and people are part of this resource allocation decision.

> Example: Agro is a smaller BU within a large corporation. Annually, Agro's management develops its business plan, largely financial, for the BU. Plans from all BUs are reviewed and discussed annually in a meeting of the unit General Managers and corporate executives. Here, resource allocations are made. Via this process, Agro's financial projections are accepted and Agro receives its capital and operating budgets. The operating budget includes R&D and marketing spending budgets, both of which are used to develop and launch new products.

The premise in these final two chapters is that, if you are a decentralized company, and there are defined business units in your company, then likely you already have in place a resource allocation scheme across BUs. That is, each BU has a budget, including R&D, marketing and capital monies and people. Thus, the question facing you is not, "how much money and people should our BU be allotted to undertake development projects?", but, "how do we spend the money and people we have been allocated?" (see Exhibit 6.1). For the smaller firm – a single BU – the question is moot: the R&D, marketing and capital budget and people resources for the company are by default the resources and money that the BU owns.

A Centralized Project Portfolio?

Although most major firms leave decentralized R&D and new product spending decisions to the BU level, there are several notable exceptions where projects from the BUs might be considered centrally:

* Large projects: In some firms, the magnitude of certain projects demands that they be reviewed at a higher level than the BU senior management. Such approvals go right to the top of the organization. An example is a new product project involving a major capital expenditure.

The result is that the BU manages a portfolio of projects, most of which are likely within its spending and approval level. Portfolio management is thus self-contained within the BU. But there is also a portfolio of major projects, which is the domain of the senior executives in the corporation. Thus there is a project portfolio management process at the top of the corporation, one which focuses on the few major projects, is centralized, and includes projects from all BUs.

* Cross-BU projects: Some projects involve several BUs, and might be dealt with centrally. For example, platform projects often cut across BU boundaries. In some firms, these multi-BU projects would simply be part of each participating BU's portfolio. In other firms, however, there may be a desire to deal with such projects centrally, thus requiring a centralized portfolio management approach, much like that described above for large projects.

Although such projects are limited to the few very largest platform projects, or the ones which involve several BUs, the point still must be made that project portfolio management *also occurs centrally*, even in decentralized firms. This chapter deals with portfolio management at the BU level. But recognize that these *same approaches* can see use *at the top* of the corporation as well in the case of centralized portfolio management.

* Inability to let go: Some senior corporate executives still want the ultimate say for all new product projects in their corporation. The paradigm is this: the BUs rate and rank their own projects and develop their own project portfolio. This prioritized list then goes to a central or corporate office for approval. The corporate executives put their blessing on certain projects, and in so doing, assign the new product budget to that BU. We did not see much evidence of this procedure in North America, but it was more common in Europe (e.g., in certain German firms we interviewed). The net result is that each BU requires its own portfolio management process; but so does the corporate management, in order to oversee all projects.

The Strategy-Process Matrix

Assume we begin from a position where top level resource allocation has occurred across BUs, using perhaps one of the corporate strategy and planning tools outlined (such as the BCG, McKinsey or GE models). At this point, the question becomes: How should the BU allocate its scarce product development resources? Note that the methods outlined below also apply both to smaller firms, where the BU is the entire company, and also to larger firms operating a centralized portfolio management scheme.

The Strategy-Process matrix provides the framework for deciding which Portfolio Management Process (PMP) is right for you (see Exhibit 6.3). The two key dimensions of this matrix are:

► whether there exists a clear and specific *new product strategy* for the BU; and

► whether the BU has a systematic *Stage-Gate or new product process*, with clearly defined *gates and criteria* in place and working.

That is, your location in the four-quadrant figure in Exhibit 6.3 decides the appropriate Portfolio Management Process (PMP) for you.

Coincidently, the two defining dimensions in Exhibit 6.3 – strategy and process – are also two of the three cornerstones of successful new product development at the business unit level[2]. The third cornerstone, ironically, is adequate resources, which is precisely what we are trying to determine how to allocate in this chapter.

Exhibit 6.3: The Strategy-Process Matrix

	No New Product Strategy	New Product Strategy with Defined Goals & Arenas
No New Product Process: **No Stage-Gate Process with Tough Gates**	**I: No Process, No NP Strategy** – A budgeting exercise: - projects selected annually based on financial merits.	**II: NP Strategy exists, but no Stage-Gate Process** - The Portfolio Review decides the portfolio at annual or semi-annual meetings; project selection based on strategy. - No gates, but occasional project reviews, which are largely information up-dates.
Systematic, Defined New Product Stage-Gate Process with Go/Kill Gates	**III: No NP Strategy, but Stage-Gate Process in place** - The portfolio is decided at the gates. - The gates must be rigorous. - The Portfolio Review is little more than an up-date of gate decisions made.	**IV: Both Stage-Gate Process & NP Strategy in place** - An integrated Portfolio Management Process (PMP). - The strategy drives the portfolio. - The gates operationalize the portfolio method. - The Portfolio Review makes course corrections.

What is New Product Strategy?

Business strategy in our context refers to the Business Unit's strategy; and new product strategy is a component of business strategy. By *business and new product strategy,* we do not mean a vaguely worded statement of intent, one that approaches a vision or mission statement. Rather we mean, at minimum, clearly defined *strategic arenas* for the BU to focus on, including how it will focus its product development efforts. These strategic arenas are defined in terms of:

- ► markets; and/or
- ► product types or categories; and/or
- ► technologies.

Strategy definition even goes as far as indicating the relative emphasis – or strategic priorities – accorded each arena of strategic focus. For example, if markets A, B and C are identified as "strategic", the relative priorities of these markets should be part of the strategy. Finally, translating this strategy into a *new product strategy for the business* begins with the strategic arenas – markets A, B and C – and shifts to the question of how to attack each strategic arena with new products. In this strategic definition, there may be:

- Decisions made on *relative spending per strategic arena.* For example, "Market A is top priority. We expect to see 50% of R&D spending aimed at Market A." This might also be translated into numbers of projects or numbers of launches expected in each strategic arena.
- Decisions or splits made in terms of the *types of projects*: For example: "Given our aggressive strategic stance in Market A, we expect to see 30% of R&D spending here on genuine new products and another 10% on fundamental research (technology development for the future); 30% will go to product modifications and improvements, and only 10% to cost reductions, while another 20% on product maintenance and fixes."
- Decisions or splits in terms of project newness, using the "newness matrix". Recall from Chapter 4 the six-cell matrix with Technology and Market Newness as the key dimensions. Projects might be classed as "defend and/or penetrate" projects through to "new businesses/new ventures" (see Exhibit 4.2).

Example: Senior management at Agro spent an exhausting session mapping out the BU's strategy. This involved reviewing the strategic mission and vision for the BU (this had already been developed in previous years and remained valid). Next a thorough SWOT analysis was undertaken. A market-by-market analysis and core competency assessment yielded a set of product type and market priorities. These were markets that Agro management really wanted to focus on, and the product lines that management wanted to target these markets with. For the majority of markets, the BU already had a presence and the majority of product types were familiar ones – existing product lines for Agro. Different technology types as possible arenas of focus were briefly discussed, but the BU was focused largely on one very successful technology where it had considerable strengths. Other technologies as arenas of focus were ruled out.

These markets and product types (product lines) were next prioritized. Then management moved to the issue of *new product strategy* for the BU, which logically evolved from the business's strategy. Management went through a difficult exercise of splitting the development budget across these prioritized markets and product lines for the BU – in effect, making forced choices, much like the Strategic Buckets Model outlined in Chapter 4. Finally, management also made some rough, idealized splits in development resources by project type: i.e., how much money for genuine new products, product improvements and modifications, product maintenance and fixes, fundamental research projects, and cost reductions (e.g., process improvements). The latter two categories – fundamental research and cost reductions – are not new product projects, but these projects do compete for the same pool of resources, and must be considered in the split. The result of this new product strategy session is summarized in Exhibit 6.4.

Exhibit 6.4: Summary of Agro's Business & NP Strategy

- BU Mission: Rapid growth: aggressively gain market share in this growing business.
- Strategy Overview: Growth via leading edge product development utilizing the BU's existing technology base; broaden distribution domestically and abroad.
- NP Goals: 75% increase in sales via new products, in the next 3 years.
- Market priorities and spending splits (see pie chart, left)
- Product Line priorities and spending splits (see pie chart, right)
- Project type splits (see pie chart, bottom)

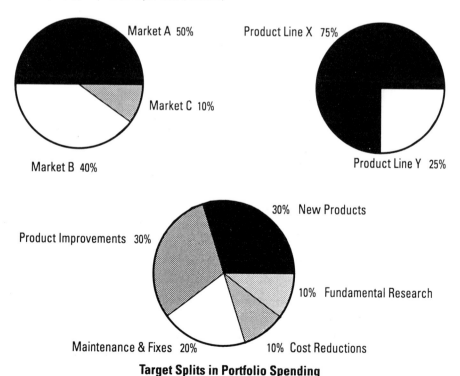

Target Splits in Portfolio Spending

Using the Strategy-Process Matrix to Decide the Portfolio Approach

Which Portfolio Management Process (PMP) is right for your company and BU? Consider the matrix in Exhibit 6.3, which is bounded by the two dimensions of strategy and process.

Quadrant IV: The Business Unit has Both a Well Defined New Product Strategy and a Systematic New Product Process, Complete with Gates

Quadrant IV in Exhibit 6.3 is a mixed blessing. It is by far the best quadrant to be in from a performance standpoint. For example, a major benchmarking study revealed that the two strongest drivers of new product performance at the business unit level were having a high quality, systematic new product process and also having a well-defined new product strategy for the business.[2] That's the good news.

The bad news is that this quadrant presents the greatest challenges – both conceptual and operational – to effective portfolio management. It is by far the most complex in that *several potentially competing decision processes* are in play. Having both a strategy and a new product or Stage-Gate process means that the Portfolio Management Process must be synchronized with both strategy and the gating process. Here's how:

In Quadrant IV, *the BU's strategy drives the portfolio decision process*. The *Portfolio Review* and models driven by strategy are the foundation for portfolio decisions. These strategically-driven reviews and decisions should occur quarterly or semi-annually*. At the same time, a *strong Stage-Gate process* is also in place, and therefore the gates must help decide the projects. The gating process is where the decisions are made on individual projects on an ongoing basis. Note that the gating process is continuous, occurring throughout the year. The two decision processes are, thus, the Portfolio Review and the Stage-Gate process. One is periodic; one is real time. Both decision processes must be fully integrated and closely linked to the BU's strategy. This integrated Portfolio Management Process is shown conceptually in Exhibit 6.5. Note how each decision process feeds the other.

Since the recommended Portfolio Management Process for Quadrant IV is the most complex of the four quadrants, we outline it in much more depth in the next chapter. But first, let's take a quick look at the other three quadrants. Note that the recommended methods in each of these three are abbreviated versions of the full-fledged PMP for Quadrant IV outlined in Chapter 7.

---

* Some firms stretch the timing and only have annual Portfolio Reviews. Experience suggests that the world moves too quickly for these annual course adjustments, and that semi-annual or even quarterly Portfolio Reviews are preferred.

Exhibit 6.5: An Overview of the Portfolio Management Process (PMP)
Linking Strategy, the Portfolio Review, and the New Product Process or Stage-Gate Model

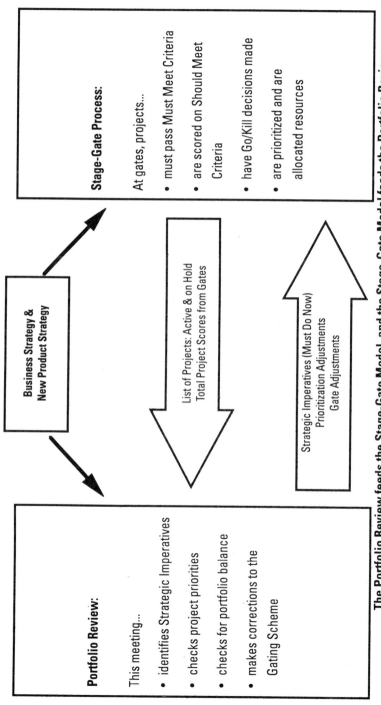

**Business Strategy &
New Product Strategy**

Stage-Gate Process:

At gates, projects...

- must pass Must Meet Criteria
- are scored on Should Meet Criteria
- have Go/Kill decisions made
- are prioritized and are allocated resources

List of Projects: Active & on Hold
Total Project Scores from Gates

Strategic Imperatives (Must Do Now)
Prioritization Adjustments
Gate Adjustments

Portfolio Review:

This meeting...

- identifies Strategic Imperatives
- checks project priorities
- checks for portfolio balance
- makes corrections to the Gating Scheme

The Portfolio Review feeds the Stage-Gate Model, and the Stage-Gate Model feeds the Portfolio Review.
Both schemes are synchronized and both are driven by Strategy.

Quadrant II: The BU has a Well-Defined Business and New Product Strategy, But No New Product Process with Gates in Place

As in Quadrant IV, the portfolio must also be driven by the BU's strategy. Indeed, lacking a new product process and Gating scheme, strategy is really the only criterion for project selection. In effect, *only half the decision-making processes* are at work, and according to our benchmarking studies, the results are inferior.[2] Decisions are made in calender time (often with long lead times), and the method fails to respond to changing circumstances and new opportunities, which tend to occur in real time. Moreover, the Portfolio Review must deal with many projects at one meeting and cuts short the informed, in-depth decision making which occurs at gates, where the focus is only on one or a few projects.

The recommended Portfolio Management Process is thus an abbreviated version of the PMP found in Quadrant IV, the left side of Exhibit 6.5. Project selection occurs at the Portfolio Review meetings held semi-annually or quarterly. Indeed, lacking tough gates, the portfolio reviews are really the *only place* where Go/Kill and resource allocation decisions are made on specific projects. At Portfolio Reviews, projects are reviewed much like in Quadrant IV above, and resource allocations are made (described later).

Although there is no Gating system in place, projects nonetheless should be reviewed periodically. But the Quadrant II project review is more a check that projects are on time, on budget, and not in trouble – in effect, project status and information sessions. These real time project reviews are not resource allocation or decision meetings.

If your business fits in Quadrant II – a defined BU strategy but no new product process – we have two recommendations:

- <u>Short term</u>: use half of the PMP scheme outlined for Quadrant IV (the left side in Exhibit 6.5), namely, the Portfolio Review to make sharper project selection decisions.
- <u>Longer term</u>: design and implement a Stage-Gate process with tough Gates and move to Quadrant IV.

Quadrant III: The BU has a Systematic Stage-Gate Process, But has No Defined Business or New Product Strategy (or the One That Exists is Vaguely Defined)

This situation is the opposite of Quadrant II. The PMP cannot be driven by the BU's business strategy, because there is none (or it is so loosely defined that it provides no real direction). Lacking a well-defined strategy, Portfolio Reviews are ineffective; so the *gates must be where the project selection and portfolio decisions are made*. That is, the gates in the new product process drive the PMP. Once again, we have half the decision processes at work, this time the right side of Exhibit 6.5. And as might be predicted, the results are inferior to those found in Quadrant IV. While gate decisions may be very astute – each project is a sound one from a financial and business standpoint – taken together, these gate decisions may be wrong. There is no attempt to stand back and look at the totality of projects; and there is no real direction to the portfolio of projects simply because there is no BU strategy to guide the Portfolio review.

The recommended approach is that, once again, an abbreviated version of the full Quadrant IV PMP be employed. Strong, effective gates are key to success here. Gates must be rigorous and employ defined criteria for making resource allocations. These Go/Kill criteria are outlined later in Chapter 7 but include Reward, Probabilities of Success, and other criteria that are proxies for reward and success likelihood. You may also have periodic portfolio meetings, but lacking strategy, these meetings are likely to be impotent, more an update of gate decisions already made.

If your business fits in Quadrant III – a new product process with gates, but no well-defined BU strategy – we have two recommendations:

- <u>Short term</u>: use half of the PMP scheme outlined for Quadrant IV (the right side in Exhibit 6.5). Employ the gates in your new product process to make sound project selection decisions.
- <u>Longer term</u>: move to Quadrant IV: Work on sharpening your business and new product strategy (see section entitled "What is New Product Strategy?" earlier in this Chapter).

Quadrant I: The BU has Neither a Business Nor a New Product Strategy – Nor Does it Have a New Product Process with Gates.

Compare being in Quadrant IV to the much simpler situation of being in Quadrant I: No new product process with gates, and no new product strategy. Lacking a strategy and lacking a stage-gate or new product process, "portfolio management" amounts to a simple annual budgeting meeting, where projects are rated and ranked largely on straightforward financial criteria: which project has the highest return, the highest NPV, and the greatest chances of commercial success? Project reviews, when held, are not decision points; rather, they are information sessions. It's a simple game in Quadrant I. The trouble is that there is no strategic direction to the portfolio, and Go/Kill decisions on specific projects are lacking. Quadrant I may not yield great results, but the decision process is straightforward!

Our recommendation:

- Move towards Quadrant IV. Start thinking about a business and new product strategy for your BU, and consider installing a Stage-Gate new product process with tough Go/Kill gates.

  <u>Example</u>: The corporation, in which Agro is a BU, had installed a five-stage, five-gate new product process several years previously. Indeed, it was the use of this Stage-Gate process that alerted management to the fact that most of the BUs really did not have a very clearly defined new product strategy for their businesses, hence, the effort to define a strategy. Thus, Agro fits into the preferred Quadrant IV: both a Stage-Gate process, as well as a business and new product strategy are in place.

Now, it is time to revisit the most complex, yet most effective, situation in Exhibit 6.5 – Quadrant IV. The next Chapter outlines in detail the Portfolio Management Process for firms in Quadrant IV. Note that the other quadrants are essentially abbreviations of what you will see in Chapter 7.

Chapter 7

Making Portfolio Management Work for You

The Portfolio Management Process for Quadrant IV

Consider the Business Unit in Quadrant IV in the Strategy-Process matrix of the last chapter (Exhibit 6.3). Here the BU has both a business and new product strategy, as well as a Stage-Gate process in place. Recall that this quadrant is the best one from a performance standpoint; it is also the most complex in terms of the portfolio management process, simply because of the various but valid decision processes which must be in harmony. In this chapter we discuss the Portfolio Management Process (PMP) in Quadrant IV in considerable detail. (Note that firms in Quadrants II and III can employ parts of the Quadrant IV PMP as noted in the previous chapter.)

The key components of the Portfolio Management Process are outlined in Exhibit 7.1 and form the major sections in this chapter. Recall that there are three important decision processes at work in Quadrant IV: the BU's business and new product strategy; the Stage-Gate process; and the Portfolio Review. In this chapter, we:

- begin at the top of Exhibit 7.1 with the role of new product strategy, how it must drive the portfolio, and how this is done in practice;
- move to the right side of Exhibit 7.1, focus on the gates in the new product process, and how the portfolio management process is operationalized at the gate decisions;
- move to the left side of Exhibit 7.1 and outline the Portfolio Review and models, how the portfolio is adjusted, and how the Portfolio Review provides corrections to the gating model in the new product process;
- bring all three together to form an integrated decision system.

Strategy Drives the Portfolio

The Portfolio Management Process is driven by strategy (see the top box in Exhibit 7.1). Why? Because strategy begins when you start spending money. Up to that point, strategy is just words on paper. Since portfolio choice is about allocating resources and making Go/Kill decisions on projects, – in short, where you spend your money – then the *portfolio choice must begin with strategy*.

After all, strategy guides and directs a business. It defines what is in or out of bounds; and it defines arenas of focus as well as their relative emphasis. The *manifestation of strategy* is decisions about where you will spend your money: the portfolio decisions.

Exhibit 7.1:   Strategy (top,center) Drives the Portfolio Management Process

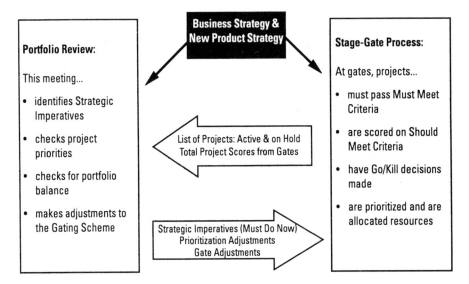

Strategy is Vital to the Portfolio Management Process (PMP)

In the PMP, strategy provides direction in three ways:

1. Strategic Fit and Importance: The BU's business and new product strategy is used as a criterion to ensure that all projects are "on strategy"; that is, all projects are within a product, market or technology area defined as *an arena of strategic focus*, and to ensure that selected projects are indeed the *strategically important* ones.

2. Breakdown of Spending: Strategy should also be used to define spending break-downs across markets, product types, technologies, and even project types (extensions versus new products; long term versus short term, etc.). In

---

Key Strategic Selection Criteria

Strategy defines the key criteria – Strategic Fit and Strategic Importance – in the gate and portfolio models. These criteria are used in a checklist or a scoring model to rate and rank projects. Sample criteria which are driven by strategy, and might be used at a gate (or at a Portfolio Review meeting) are:

Must Meet:
• Does the project fit our strategy? That is, is it within a product, market or technology arena that we have defined in our business strategy?

                                Yes ____   No ____
Here, a "No" kills the project ... culls it out of the project pipeline.

Should Meet (these are scored 1-5 or 0-10):
• To what degree is the project "on strategy" (fits our strategy)?
     (0=not at all; 10=perfectly fits strategy)
• What is the strategic importance of the project – how important is this project to the business? (0=not at all; 10=essential from a strategic viewpoint)

the section on strategy in the last chapter, we saw how a defined new product strategy for the BU should not only define "what is on strategy" but should even go as far as defining desired spending splits along key dimensions. For example, strategy should define spending priorities and splits in terms of:

- strategic arenas of focus (product types, markets or technology areas);
- project types (genuine new products versus modifications, versus tweaks and product maintenance projects).

In this way, strategic buckets of funds – or envelopes of money – can be pre-established (desired levels of spending in different areas) which should mirror the business's new product strategy.

Recall from Chapter 4 that these first two points – strategic fit and importance, and breakdown of spending reflecting strategic priorities – are subtly different. For example, a portfolio can have every project consistent with the business's strategy, yet the breakdown of the spending is skewed too much towards one market or to one product line. When all projects fit the BU's strategy, and when the spending breakdown across project types reflects the BU's strategic priorities, then we have *strategic alignment*.

3. <u>Strategic Imperatives</u>: Strategy may also define some "must do" projects right away (i.e., unless there exist some other killer variables, let's give these projects a Go and top priority). These "must do" projects are called *strategic imperatives*. For example, if the business's strategy were to expand aggressively in one key market, and one new product project was identified as pivotal to this expansion, the decision here might be an immediate Go. Alternately, if another market were defined as a strategic priority, and a key product improvement was needed just to defend share in that market, once again a "strategic decision" might be made: an immediate Go!

The New Product Process – Gating is Also Key for the PMP

The second vital decision making system in the PMP is the new product Stage-Gate process, specifically the gates (the right side of Exhibit 7.2). In an effective new product process, gates are the quality control checkpoints. Gates are where senior management put their blessing on projects; and gates are where the resources are allocated for a day-to-day basis throughout the year. Thus, the PMP is operationalized at gate meetings on individual projects. Note that these individual decisions on specific projects must be integrated into a greater whole, the portfolio. View the individual projects as fingers, the portfolio of projects is the fist!

Getting the gates right is a difficult challenge, so we devote a major section of this final chapter to gates. Here is a road map of this critical section:

1. First, we introduce the concept of a *Stage-Gate Process* and provide a brief outline.
2. Next, we propose a scoring model and checklist scheme to *achieve the three goals* of effective portfolio management, namely value maximization; balance; and strategic alignment.
3. *Gate criteria* – the items you can use to score, rate and rank projects – are outlined, with samples provided.
4. How gates indeed *achieve the three goals* is summarized next.
5. How gates consider *balance* and *strategic alignment* is outlined, a difficult but important issue.
6. Next, we discuss *correcting the balance* at the gate decision points, and outline the details of correcting mechanisms ... so that gate decisions move the portfolio towards the ideal.
7. *Prioritizing projects and resource allocation* is the next topic. Here we view the gates as a two-part decision process.
8. A final and controversial issue dealt with in this section is just *how firm are resource commitments* made to projects?

This road map for this section on gates is sketched in Exhibit 7.3.

Exhibit 7.2:   An Important Facet of PMP is the Gates in a Stage-Gate Process

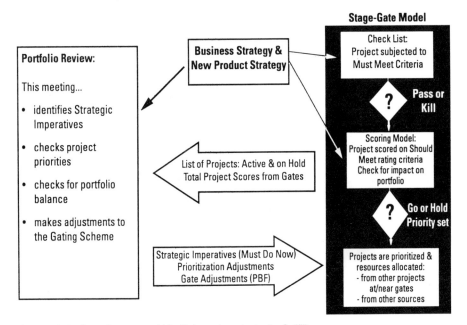

The gates in the Stage-Gate process (right side) are where day-to-day Go/Kill decisions are made, and are an important facet of the total Portfolio Management Process.

Stage-Gate Processes

A Stage-Gate process is a road map to drive new product projects from idea through to launch.[1] A typical Stage-Gate process is shown in Exhibit 7.4. The process illustrated in the exhibit has five stages, including familiar ones such as Development, Validation and Launch. Preceding each stage is a gate – a Go/Kill decision point, where management meets to decide on the merits of the project, and whether or not it should receive funding or resources for the next stage. These decision-makers or "gatekeepers" are usually the senior managers in the BU, especially at Gate 3 onward, where resource commitments increase.

Numerous companies have adopted Stage-Gate and similar new product processes including: Exxon Chemical, P&G, GTE, Hoechst, SC Johnsons Wax, Polaroid, Corning, Dow Chemicals, Reckitt & Colman, International Paper, Union Camp, Lego, Rohm & Haas, St Gobain, Carlsberg, Pillsbury, American Express, Royal Bank of Canada, and many others.

Exhibit 7.3:   A Road Map of the Gating Section in this Chapter

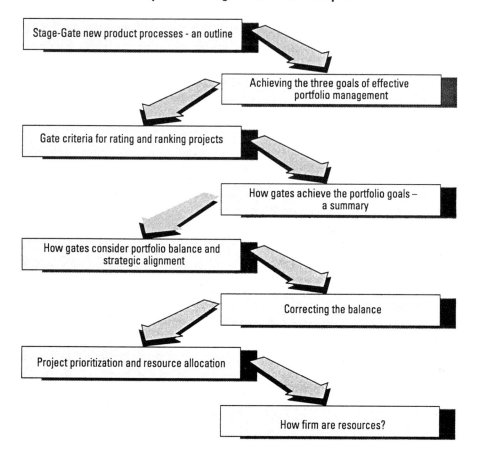

Stage-Gate new product processes - an outline

Achieving the three goals of effective portfolio management

Gate criteria for rating and ranking projects

How gates achieve the portfolio goals – a summary

How gates consider portfolio balance and strategic alignment

Correcting the balance

Project prioritization and resource allocation

How firm are resources?

Exhibit 7.4: An Overview of a Generic Stage-Gate Process

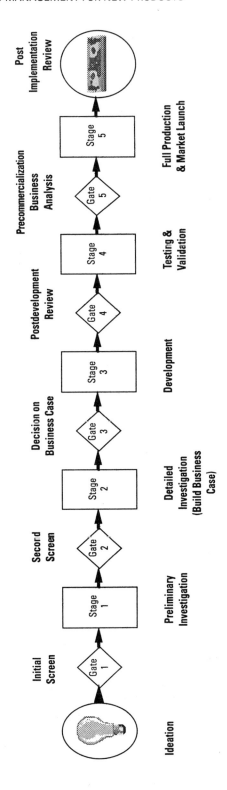

There are five stages plus the idea stage. Each stage is preceded by a Go/Kill decision point or "gate".

Adapted from *Winning at New Products* by Robert G. Cooper
Stage-Gate is a tradename of R.G. Cooper.

Stage-Gate New Product Processes: An Outline

A Stage-Gate Process is the game plan to drive projects from the idea stage through to launch. Embedded within the process are *gate decision points*, where the day-to-day Go/Kill decisions are made on projects.

> Example: Recall that Agro's new product process is a five-stage, five-gate scheme, very similar to the one in Exhibit 7.4. The gates were working effectively, according to management, culling out the poor projects. But an overall Portfolio Management Process was missing that took a more holistic and integrated view of all projects.

At some gate in the Stage-Gate Process, resource commitments become sufficiently large that prioritization must take place. Prior to this gate, projects are reasonably small and ill-defined so that putting them into the PMP – subjecting them to a portfolio prioritization – does not make much sense. Either the data on each project is very uncertain (e.g., financial projections, and estimates of future resource requirements, timing and success likelihoods), the resource commitments are too small, or both.

Assume that the Portfolio Management Process kicks in at the pivotal "Go to Development" decision point, or Gate 3 in the scheme in Exhibit 7.4*. This means:

- Projects are prioritized starting at this gate.
- From this gate onward, resource commitments are more or less firm.

From this Gate onward, one rule might be that the project continues to receive resources, as long as it doesn't shoot itself. If the project meets all deliverables, stays on its timeline, and continues to meet all successive gate criteria, it remains a Go and the resource commitments remain in place.

Note that different businesses employ *different rules* regarding the firmness of resource commitments. Later in this chapter, we will see some sample rules in the box entitled "How Firm Are Resource Commitments?". The rule we recommend is the one just cited above: Once past a certain gate, resource commitments are firm, as long as the project remains a good one, and continues to meet all criteria at successive gates.

Achieving the Three Goals of Effective Portfolio Management

The gate decision rules must be deliberately constructed to achieve three portfolio goals. Recall from Chapters 2, 3 and 4 what these goals were:

- *Maximization of value* to the business. Here, value is measured in many ways (see Chapter 2);
- *Proper balance* of projects; for example, between high risk and low risk, between high payoff and more modest projects (see Chapter 3); and,
- *Strategic alignment,* where projects and spending breakdowns are consistent with the business's strategy (see Chapter 4).

---

*   This "kick in" point may vary by company. For example, some firms spend considerable resources in Stage 2, the stage before Development, so that Gate 2 is the point at which the portfolio model kicks in and project prioritization begins.

How can these three potentially *conflicting goals* be realized in the same decision model? And, how can projects be quantitatively rank ordered from best to worst? Scoring models are a preferred tool here. When multiple goals exist, scoring models are particularly suited to *rating projects* as well as *ranking them* in order to yield a prioritized list. In practice, we recommend that the gates should first use a checklist scheme (yes/no) to provide an initial culling, followed by a scoring model to deal with the multiple portfolio goals defined above.

- The checklist is used to cull out obvious misfit projects; for example, those that are way "off strategy".
- The scoring model is then used to rate and rank projects against the multiple goals noted above.

Gate Criteria for Rating and Ranking Projects

The checklist and scoring model scheme should consider specific criteria in several broad areas:

- Strategic – both strategic fit and strategic importance (these were highlighted in the box "Key Strategic Selection Criteria").
- Reward – what is the size of the prize (e.g., NPV if successful)?[*]
- Probability of success (commercial and/or technical).
- Balance: Does this project move us closer to the ideal portfolio (in terms of balance across markets, technologies, product types, project types and, most importantly, spending breakdowns that are consistent with strategy)?

In practice, a much longer list of factors is built into the scoring model and checklist – factors such as Product Advantage, Market Attractiveness and Synergies. These are simply proxies for Reward and/or Probability of Success, hence, the long list of items used in the typical gate scoring model. Exhibit 7.5 gives a sample set of Must and Should Meet criteria for the "Go to Development" decision point. This is the gate where the portfolio scheme may kick in and serious project prioritization begins (Gate 3 in Exhibit 7.4).

> Example: Agro uses a combination checklist and scoring model at the various gates in its Stage-Gate process. Gate 3 is a vital decision point, where the project becomes a full-fledged Development project. The Gate 3 gate-keepers are the senior people, and the meeting is chaired by the General Manager of the business. The checklist and scoring models used at Gate 3 are quite similar to the samples shown in Exhibit 7.5.

---

[*]   There exists debate about whether Reward should be considered after or before probabilities of success have been factored in. Some firms use "most likely" but single point estimates to determine the NPV; others use a probability model (e.g., a decision tree) with various possible outcomes and probabilities of occurring; still others use a Monte Carlo simulation model which yields an expected NPV as well as a probability distribution around it; finally some companies simply use a "risk adjusted NPV" obtained by using a higher discount rate in the case of riskier projects. See Chapter 3.

Consider a real project of Agro's at the Gate 3 decision point, namely Bio-55. The project has had a small two-person team working on it for the last four months. Market studies have been completed; some preliminary technical (laboratory) work has been undertaken, enough to establish a reasonable likelihood of technical feasibility. And the Business Case has been built. The product has been defined (target market, product benefits, price point, technical requirements and high level specs); the project justified, namely the financial analysis and business rationale; and the project plan or action plan mapped out for the next stages of the project.

At Gate 3, senior management reviews the Bio-55 project against a set of Must Meet criteria (as in Exhibit 7.5). Bio-55 passes all of them: there are no negative votes here. Next, the project is scored on the Should Meet items. Here a 0-10 scoring scheme is used, and scores are averaged in an unweighted fashion to yield Factors; and Factors are added to yield a Total Project Score. In Agro's scheme all factors must clear a minimum hurdle, and so must the Total Project Score. Exhibit 7.6 shows the scoring model results accorded Bio-55. Out of a possible 60 points, the project scores 45.5, for a Total Project Score of 76%. The Bio-55 project scores very well and clears all the Gate 3 hurdles, including the 60% hurdle on the Total Project Score. It looks like a Go – or is it?

How Gates Achieve the Portfolio Goals: A Summary

Here's how the gates achieve the desired goals of maximum value, balance and strategic alignment via a checklist and a scoring scheme:

- Goal 1. Maximization of the portfolio value:

  Many criteria in the checklist and scoring model deal with the value of the project to the corporation. In sample criteria shown in Exhibit 7.5, these "value to the corporation" items include criteria dealing with strategic importance, product advantage, market attractiveness, financial reward (or payoff) and probability of success. Projects that score high on these criteria tend to achieve high overall total project scores via the scoring model, and most likely pass the gate hurdles easily.

- Goals 2 & 3. Properly balanced and strategically aligned portfolio:

  This is an important concept, often missed by the firms we studied:
  - *Strategically aligned* means all projects are "on strategy"; and that the spending breakdown across projects is consistent with the business's priorities and strategies.
  - *Properly balanced* means that we have the appropriate breakdown in spending (or numbers of projects) across markets, product types, technologies and project types.

These two goals (2 and 3) go hand in hand.

Exhibit 7.5: Sample Gate 3 Criteria – the "Go to Development" Decision Point

Must Meet Criteria (must yield "Yes" answers):
- Strategic Alignment (fits BU's strategy)
- Existence of Market Need (of sufficient size)
- Reasonable Likelihood of Technical Feasibility
- Product Advantage (unique customer benefits; value for money)
- Meets SHEL Policies of Company (safety, health, environmental, legal)
- Positive Return vs. Risk
- No Show-Stoppers (absence of killer variables)

Should Meet (scored):

Strategic:
- degree to which project fits the BU's strategy
- strategic importance

Product Advantage:
- unique customer benefits
- meets customer needs better
- good value for money for customer

Market Attractiveness:
- market size
- margins in this market
- market growth
- competitive situation

Synergies (Leverages Core Competencies):
- marketing synergies
- technological synergies
- manufacturing/processing synergies

Technical Feasibility:
- technical gap
- technical complexity
- technical uncertainty

Risk Vs. Return:
- expected profitability (magnitude; e.g. NPV)
- return (e.g., IRR)
- payback period
- certainty of return/profit estimates
- low cost & fast to do

These Should Meet items above are scored (e.g. 1-5 or 0-10) and added (in a weighted or unweighted fashion) to yield Factor Scores. The Factor Scores must clear hurdles. They are also added (weighted or unweighted) to yield the Total Project Score.

Exhibit 7.6:   Gate 3 Scores for Agro's Bio-55 Project

Should Meet (scored 1-10):

Strategic:	Out of 10	
• degree to which project aligns with BU's strategy	8	
• strategic importance	7	Strategic = 7.5

Product Advantage:		
• unique customer benefits	9	
• meets customer needs better	8	
• good value for money	7	Product Advantage = 8.0

Market Attractiveness:		
• market size	9	
• margins in this market	7	
• market growth	7	
• competitive situation	5	Market Attractiveness = 7.0

Synergies (Leverages Core Competencies):		
• marketing synergies	6	
• technological synergies	8	
• manufacturing/processing synergies	7	Synergies = 7.0

Technical Feasibility:		
• technical gap	9	
• technical complexity	6	
• technical uncertainty	9	Tech Feasibility = 8.0

Risk Vs. Return:		
• expected profitability (magnitude; e.g. NPV)	9	
• return (e.g. IRR)	9	
• payback period	9	
• certainty of return/profit estimates	7	
• low cost & fast to do	6	Risk/Return = 8.0

Total Project Score = 45.5 out of a possible 60 points, which is 76%.

How Gates Consider Portfolio Balance and Strategic Alignment

Balance and strategic alignment are achieved at gates in four ways:

1. First, as part of the BU's business and new product strategy, strategic buckets should have been defined (see box entitled "Strategic Buckets"). At minimum we recommend an a priori split in terms of project types: genuine new and improved products, product fixes, product maintenance, process improvements, and cost reductions. Within each bucket, similar projects can be rated, ranked and prioritized against each other. The strategic buckets approach ensures that the balance of spending on projects more or less mirrors spending priorities as dictated by the BU's strategy. The end result is three or four lists of prioritized projects, each within a bucket.

2. The *strategic criteria* in the checklist and scoring model are designed to deliberately favor *strategically important* and *high strategic fit* projects. As noted above, these strategic criteria might be either Must Meet or Should Meet criteria (or both*).

The use of a checklist and a scoring model at gates based on the sample criteria in Exhibit 7.5 means that all "off strategy" projects will be culled out; and the remaining

---

Strategic Buckets

The Strategic Buckets approach forces spending breakdowns to mirror strategic priorities. In developing your BU business and new product strategy, recall from the "Strategy" section that decisions should be made about desired spending levels or splits in terms of some or all of the following (see Agro example in the last chapter, Exhibit 6.4):

- split by strategic arena (e.g. market, product types or lines, or technology arenas);
- types of projects (e.g. new products versus minor changes);
- project newness (across the cells in the newness matrix).

These desired splits, derived from strategic priorities, can be used as a point of comparison at Portfolio Review meetings. For example, how does your actual spending breakdown compare with the desired split? If there are gaps, then course corrections can be made.

These splits can be used *more aggressively* as well via a Strategic Buckets approach (see Chapter 4). These desired splits are translated into buckets of money for different types of projects. The result is three or four prioritized lists of projects – one for each bucket.

Example: Agro's management did develop desired splits of spending across arenas, such as markets and product types (see the pie charts in Exhibit 6.4). But they chose not to force these spending splits by establishing strategic buckets. One dimension was a concern: types of projects. Here Agro did develop five strategic buckets and assigned resources to each:

- genuine new products;
- product improvements;
- product fixes, maintenance and product necessity work;
- cost reductions and process improvements; and
- fundamental "knowledge build" research.

Projects within each of these five categories compete against each other; but there is no competition among projects between buckets, so that the overall split of spending is dictated by the strategic buckets.

---

*   For example, Strategic Fit could be a Yes/No criterion; it could also be a scaled question as a Should Meet item, as shown in Exhibit 7.5.

projects in the portfolio will be strongly weighted towards very high strategic fit and strategically important ones. So strategy is built into the gates via the Must Meet and Should Meet criteria.

3. At gate meetings, the portfolio lists and maps are reviewed. The question is posed: How does a Go decision on this project impact the total portfolio? The approach here is to discuss the portfolio of projects – the list of active projects, prioritized; and the various maps or charts which display the portfolio – with and without the new proposed project. Note that discussion should focus *only on the impact* that the addition of this one project at the gate will have on the portfolio. This is *not the venue to address the total portfolio of projects*. Opening up this discussion at every gate meeting would lead to chaos!

4. The final way the gates yield a *strategically aligned* and *properly balanced portfolio* is via building in a *correction factor* into the gate decision model. This is done by adding certain gate criteria, or by adjusting the scoring model score, or by adjusting the minimum acceptable hurdles. These manoeuvres are all designed to favor certain types of projects; namely, projects that bring the portfolio closer to the ideal balance and closer to the desired spending breakdown.

Correcting the Balance

Correcting the balance via the "correction factor" can be achieved in one of three ways, all variations on the same theme:

- Adjust the hurdles: The hurdles on some Must Meet criteria, or the Total Project Score hurdle, can be shifted, as does Reckitt & Colman (see Chapter 5, Exhibit 5.2). For example, the financial or scoring model hurdles can be relaxed for projects that are highly desired in the portfolio*, and increased for project types that are over-represented. The end result is that gate decisions will be tilted slightly in favor of desired projects, and over time, the portfolio imbalance will be corrected.

- Add criteria: Another way to build in the correction factor is to add several criteria to the scoring model that ask the question: *Does this project move us closer to the ideal portfolio?* Projects that are desired score more points, obtain a higher Total Project Score, hence, have a higher likelihood of passing the gate.

- Adjust the Score: This method is what we recommend for its operational simplicity ... it's simple and it works! We adjust the scores in the scoring model via a Portfolio Balance Factor (PBF). The Portfolio Balance Factor is determined from the answer to the question: *Does this project move us closer to the ideal portfolio?* The PBF is simply multiplied by the Total Project Score to tilt the scales in favor of desired projects (and against those

---

* For example, by decreasing the financial hurdle rate from, say, 25% ROI to 20% for certain desired types of projects.

which we already have too many of).**

Example: In Agro's scoring model at Gate 3, the minimum hurdle is normally 60 points out of possible 100. If the portfolio were totally in balance and strategically aligned, the PBF would be 1.0. However, suppose it was decided a priori by management that there are too many projects aimed at Market C and not enough aimed at Market B. The PBF works this way: for Market B projects – which are very much needed – the PBF is increased to 1.1 and thus the resulting Total Project Score multiplied by 1.1. For Market C projects – there are too many of these in the portfolio already – the PBF drops to, say 0.9. In effect, the method favors Market B projects and penalizes Market C projects. This means that unless Market C projects are really good ones, they fail the gate.

As it turned out, the Bio-55 project was in a market area, namely Market B, deemed vital to Agro – a high priority market. Recall that management had developed a desired split in R&D spending across markets via its strategic exercise (see Exhibit 6.4, last chapter). It was thought that Market B should receive about 40% of spending. Currently Market B only accounts for about 28% of spending, so that a *considerable gap* exists. Thus the PBF for projects aimed at Market B (such as Bio-55) was set at 1.1. Multiplying Bio-55's total project score of 76% by 1.1 now makes Bio-55 an even more attractive project with a Total Project Score of 84%, simply because Bio-55 drives the portfolio closer to achieving strategic alignment.

But where and how does one decide in the first place that there are too many of Market C and not enough Market B projects? Surely not at each and every gate meeting – that would be too cumbersome. Defining gaps and establishing PBF values is the role of the Portfolio Review in the next major section of this chapter.

Project Prioritization and Resource Allocation

The outcome of the checklist and scoring model exercise at the gate is a decision: the project is either a Kill – it fails the criteria and hurdles; or a Pass. Merely being a Pass does not guarantee that the project will be immediately resourced, however. There is still the question of finding the resources for the project.

The gate meeting is conceptually a two part decision process (Exhibit 7.7). The first part rates and scores the project, leading to a Kill or Pass decision. The second facet of the gate meeting deals with prioritization and the decision to allocate resources to the Go projects.

Assume that the project at the gate review passes the Must Meet criteria, and its total project score clears the hurdles for the Should Meet criteria. Will it be resourced? And where will the resources come from? These are the questions for the second part of the gate meeting (the second diamond in Exhibit 7.7).

** The use of this multiplicative PBF is almost the same as *adjusting the hurdles to favor certain projects*, but a little easier to use when ranking projects; and it is similar to *adding a few criteria* to the scoring model, except that it is multiplicative rather than additive.

Exhibit 7.7: The Two-Step Decision Process at Gates

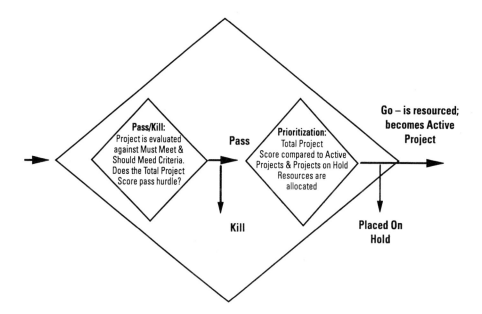

Pass/Kill:
Project is evaluated against Must Meet & Should Meed Criteria. Does the Total Project Score pass hurdle?

Pass

Prioritization:
Total Project Score compared to Active Projects & Projects on Hold Resources are allocated

Go – is resourced; becomes Active Project

Kill

Placed On Hold

The gatekeepers face two choices here: either they resource the project – it becomes (or continues as) an active or Go project; or they place it on Hold. Projects in the Hold tank are good projects; it's just that resources are scarce and other projects are better.

At this point, the project under review must be compared to other projects – both active projects already underway as well as projects in the Hold tank. If the project under consideration rates better than projects in the Hold tank, and equal to active projects, then it should be resourced. The Total Project Score from the scoring model should be used to make this comparison. Recall that this Total Project Score captures the value of the project to the business (strategic importance and fit, reward, and probability of success) as well as how well the project fits into the total portfolio.

If the decision is to resource the project, then the gatekeepers must find the resources. Usually these are not just lying around waiting to be allocated: people invariably are very busy on other, very worthwhile projects and tasks! And many companies have a rule that other projects cannot be de-prioritized between gates just to fund a relative new-comer. Nonetheless, resources must be found. The potential sources of resources that gatekeepers must investigate include:

- resources already assigned to the project under review, which would have been spun off had this project been stopped;
- resources available in the very near future from projects completing certain phases, where certain project people are no longer required on that team;

► resources from projects in trouble which should be shut down or curtailed (this could entail an "unscheduled" gate meeting in order to kill a project in trouble);

► resources from projects soon to be facing a gate meeting (note that one rule is that although resources are firm between gates, at gates, each project is reviewed and may indeed be killed, thereby freeing resources for other projects);

► new resources (e.g., new hires, transfers, people between assignments); and,

► outside sources (e.g., other divisions, corporate labs, strategic partners, universities, outside labs, consultants or contract people).

If the resources cannot be found, then the project is placed in the Hold tank. This should happen only after every effort has been found to support this worthwhile, high scoring project.

Example: Agro's Bio-55 achieved a very positive adjusted score of 84% at Gate 3 – a score which placed is above other projects in the Hold tank, and indeed among the better projects on the active list. So the decision was Go. Indeed, the decision was a strong Go, and maximum resources were allocated. Resources were acquired from several sources: First, the two-person team already on the project was assigned to continue as key team players. Other technology players were added from another project, soon to be entering the Launch phase, where their services would not be required full time. Finally, a project with several people assigned was approaching a Gate 4 meeting, and might be cancelled, potentially freeing up a few more people for Bio-55.

How Firm are Resources?

A thorny question is this: just how firm are the resources, once they are committed to a project (see issue number 7, Chapter 5)? Our recommendation is that each business develop its own rule on resource commitment. At one extreme is the "resources are infinitely flexible" paradigm. This means that resource commitments are certainly not firm, and that senior management can move resources from one project to the next at will. At the other extreme is the "resource commitments are kept" paradigm, which is equally problematic: this is a good way to throw a lot of money at projects in trouble. Between these extremes, there are a number of common-sense rules. See the box entitled "How Firm Are Resource Commitments" for some examples.

Example: In Bio-55's case, resources were committed at Gate 3. These allocations were firm, provided the project remained a good one. Thus the project leader could plan confidently. She was well aware, however, that the project could fail at Gate 4 and be cancelled or de-prioritized.

So much for gates and decisions on individual projects – the fingers. Now let's turn to the fist – the portfolio of all projects considered together.

How Firm are Resource Commitments?

Different firms employ different rules of thumb. Here are some samples:

1. Resources committed at gates are infinitely flexible. In short, if a better project comes along, resources can be readily stripped from projects already underway. There is no such thing as a "firm resource commitment"!

2. Resources are only firm between one gate and the next. At every gate, the project is "up for grabs" and can be reprioritized, or even put on Hold, if it does not score as high as other projects in the pipe or those in the Hold tank. If the project gets into trouble between gates – shoots itself – an immediate gate review is called, and the resources may be taken away from the project (e.g., it is killed). Exxon Chemical employs this rule.

3. Resources are firm, starting at a certain gate. That is, as long as the project continues a good one – meets timelines, budgets, and all successive gate criteria – then the project leader and team can expect continued funding. Even if a newer and better project comes along, top management will resist the temptation to strip resources from the already approved project. As in Rule 2 above, if the project gets into trouble between gates, an immediate gate review is called, and the resources may be taken away from the project. The NSD division of GTE employs this rule.

4. Resources are firm, starting at a certain gate. The project is expected to pass all successive gates, thus, these gate reviews are largely perfunctory. That is, once the project is commissioned, the expectation is that it will reach the marketplace.

We recommend Rule 3, followed by 2 above. Rule 1 – infinitely flexible resources – may be great in economic theory (efficient allocation of resources), but plays havoc with project teams and morale. Moreover, newcomer projects always look better than ones that are three-quarters complete, hence, resources tend to be stripped from the latter. Taken to an extreme, no project ever gets completed! Rule 4 is seen far too often. It is the express-train approach where gates become "project reviews" but there's never any intention or will to stop a mediocre project. This rule results in many poor projects reaching the marketplace, and mis-allocation of scarce and valuable resources.

The Portfolio Review

The Portfolio Review is a holistic review of all projects in the portfolio, and is held twice per year, perhaps even quarterly. This review takes the inputs and decisions made at gates and makes needed adjustments both to the portfolio of projects and to the gating decision process (the left side of Exhibit 7.8).

Ideally, the Portfolio Review should be merely a *course correction*. If the gating process and gate criteria are well-designed and effectively applied, the portfolio meeting should not result in a major adjustment to the portfolio. The hope here is that the gates are working well and doing a pretty good job of selecting and prioritizing projects throughout the year. Thus, instead of massive re-allocations of resources occurring at the Portfolio Review – a 90 degree turn in direction – the desire is to have minor corrections to the portfolio of projects – a 5 degree change. Recall that maximizing the value, strategic fit and importance, and portfolio balance are very much the key criteria at the gates. Hence, projects selected at gates should be fairly good ones.

Exhibit 7.8: The Portfolio Review (PMP)

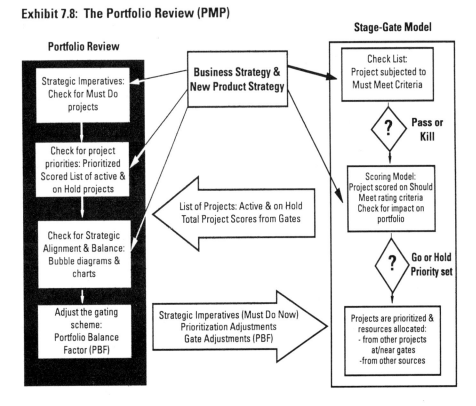

The Portfolio Review (left side) provides a holistic view of the portfolio of all projects considered together, and is a key part of the Total Portfolio Management Process.

Steps in the Portfolio Review

This Portfolio Review or course correction, which ideally takes place several times per year, involves the following steps (see Exhibit 7.8):

1. Strategic Imperatives: first, there is a review of the BU's strategy and an identification of any Strategic Imperatives; that is, projects which are absolutely essential to achieving the strategy.

    Example: Agro management have a Portfolio Review meeting twice a year. At the December Portfolio Review, each of the key strategic thrusts and arenas was discussed. One question focused on the need to move ahead right now with any projects essential to the BU's strategy. At this meeting no such Go decisions were made. There were no strategically vital projects currently on Hold.

2. Check Project Priorities – The Prioritized Scored List: Next, there is a check that projects are ranked and prioritized appropriately: that the projects scoring highest on the key criteria – those with the greatest value to the corporation – are indeed being given top priority and maximum resources (versus, say, lower

priority projects or those in the Hold tank). If too many projects in the Hold tank score higher than active projects, something is wrong!

The key criteria at the Portfolio Review *are the same as those at the gate* (reward, probabilities, strategic fit and importance). Indeed, the *same scoring model* should be used, but this time across all projects together. The scores or ratings given to projects at their most recent gate meetings are used at the Portfolio Review. For some projects, these scores are updated in the event of new information acquired since the gate.

The Total Project Score for each project becomes the ranking criterion for use in a Prioritized Scored List. This Prioritized Scored List is simply a rank ordered list of active and on hold projects (see example in Exhibit 7.9).

> Example: Agro's list of active and funded new product projects past Gate 3 – the Prioritized Scored List – was reviewed (see Exhibit 7.9). In Agro's case, recall that a priori, management had split resources into five strategic buckets. One of these buckets was for genuine new products. (Exhibit 7.9 shows these projects; a similar list rank ordered list – not shown – was prepared for product modifications and improvements). The exhibit also shows projects in the Hold tank; these are shown below the line. The projects are rank-ordered on this Prioritized Scored List according to the Total Project Score. Note that these scores have been adjusted by the PBF in order to push projects towards the top that bring the portfolio closer to strategic alignment and proper balance. For example, the project *Legume N-2,* with an initial score of 70, might not have made the active list, except for the adjustment via the PBF, which drives its score up to a respectable 77.

Exhibit 7.9:   Agro's Prioritized Scored List of Active and On Hold Projects (New Products Bucket Only)

Project Name	Rank (Priority Level)	Total Project Score	Portfolio Balance Factor	Adjusted Total Project Score
Soya-44	1	80	1.10	88
Encapsulated	2	82	1.00	82
Legume N-2	3	70	1.10	77
Spread-Ease	4	75	1.00	75
Charcoal-Base	5	80	0.90	72
Projects On Hold				
N2-Fix	1	80	1.00	80
Slow-Release	2	70	1.10	77
Multi-Purpose	3	75	0.90	68
etc.	etc.			

The Adjusted Total Project Score is the Total Project Score multiplied by the correction factor, the Portfolio Balance Factor (PBF).

Management now checks to ensure that projects at the top of the list are indeed receiving the right priorities in terms of resource allocation, and that the active projects have higher scores than projects on Hold. Several projects on Hold have excellent scores, namely *N2-Fix* and *Slow-Release*. Indeed, they both have better adjusted scores than some active and funded projects, specifically *Spread-Ease* and *Charcoal-Base*. But both *Spread-Ease* and *Charcoal-Base* are well on their way through Testing and moving toward Launch. Both still have good scores and continue to clear the gate hurdles. So the decision is to continue with *Spread-Ease* and *Charcoal-Base*, and to seek resources for the two top-rated Hold projects, *N-2 Fix* and *Slow-Release*, resourcing these as soon as people become available.

3. Check for Balance and Alignment: Here the key question is: When all the active or Go projects are considered together, is the resulting portfolio strategically aligned and properly balanced? Recall from above that:

    ▶   strategically aligned means all projects are on strategy, and the spending breakdown across projects is consistent with the business's priorities and strategies; and

    ▶   properly balanced means that we have the appropriate breakdown in spending (or numbers of projects) across markets, product types, technologies and project types.

Various visual displays are recommended to portray the existing portfolio of active projects and to check for balance. Our study of portfolio methods in use revealed that visual displays were best suited to portray balance in the portfolio (see Chapter 3). Here are the more useful charts:

• Bubble diagrams: Reward versus risk. Here the vertical axis is the probability of technical success; the horizontal axis is the reward measured via NPV (already adjusted for commercial risks); and the size of the circles denotes the magnitude of spending on that project (Exhibit 7.10A). Better yet, if there is a fear of over-emphasis of financial measures (such as NPV), try a risk/reward diagram where the axes are qualitative and derived from the gate scoring model in Exhibit 7.5:

    ▶   Reward is the horizontal axis, and is comprised of a weighted addition of: Market Attractiveness, Risk vs. Return and Strategic.

    ▶   Probability of success is the vertical Axis, and is made up of the weighted addition of: Product Advantage, Synergies (Leverages Core Competencies) and Probability of Technical Success.

Such a bubble diagram, shown in Exhibit 7.10B, combines the methods used by Reckitt & Colman (scored axes: Exhibit 3.7) and Specialty Minerals (scored axes based on their gate scoring model) with ADL's non-financial approach to estimating Reward.

An alternative version of this bubble diagram is to adapt the 3M approach by depicting certainty of estimates via the size of the circles (small circles denote very certain estimates; large circles or ellipses portray widely varying and hence uncertain estimates – see Exhibit 7.11).

Example: The bubble diagrams for Agro in Exhibits 7.10A and B and 7.11 portray the risk-reward snap-shot of the portfolio. Note that these exhibits show two types of projects from two strategic buckets, both new product projects as well as product improvements and modifications. Agro has three clear Pearls – high reward, high probability projects. Not surprisingly, they were also at the top of the Prioritized Scored List of new product projects in Exhibit 7.9. One new product project is a longshot, or Oyster, namely *Legume N-2*. Bread and Butter projects are numerous, and include one low-risk major new product with a modest reward *(Charcoal-Base)* and one major *(Slow-Release-4)*, a product improvement on an existing Agro product. Smaller projects in this Bread and Butter quadrant are A, B, C and D. All are product improvements. There is one White Elephant, *Vigor-B*, a product improvement which has run into trouble. This project began life with a higher likelihood of success, but technical problems arose and the project had drifted into the White Elephant quadrant.

Overall, management's assessment of the distribution of projects in the bubble diagram of Exhibit 7.10A was positive. The risk-reward pattern showed no obvious patterns for concern. For example, one longshot Oyster project was deemed about right. The one White Elephant was discussed, and the decision was to call for an immediate gate meeting for an imminent Go/Kill decision. Within weeks, *Vigor-B* was killed.

The bubble diagram in Exhibits 7.10B and 7.11 show essentially the same information as Exhibit 7.10A. In Exhibit 7.10B, Reward is portrayed in non-financial terms with both axes derived from the scoring model results; and Exhibit 7.11 shows uncertainties around estimates, illustrated by the sizes and shapes of the ellipses.

- Pie charts: These charts show splits in resources being spent, or numbers of projects, across key dimensions, compared against the ideal or desired spending pattern. These charts provide a check for *strategic alignment*. Spending displays can be broken down by:
  - product type, product category or product line (see left pie chart, Exhibit 7.12).
  - market or segment (right pie chart, Exhibit 7.12).
  - types of projects: genuine new products, modifications and improvement, customer request projects, and product maintenance projects or fixes (bottom pie chart, Exhibit 7.12).
  - project newness via the "newness" matrix (not shown; see Exhibit 4.2 in Chapter 4 for an example).

Example: Agro's project spending breakdowns in Exhibit 7.12 reveal *gaps between actual spending and desired spending* splits. Recall that management had specified desired spending splits as part of the strategic planning exercise (see Exhibit 6.4 in the previous chapter for desired breakdowns for both new product projects as well as product improvements).

Exhibit 7.10A: Agro's Risk-Return Bubble Diagram   (2 buckets)

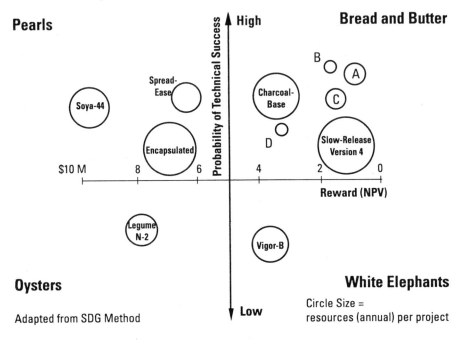

Pearls

Bread and Butter

Probability of Technical Success — High / Low

B A C

Spread-Ease

Soya-44

Charcoal-Base

D

Encapsulated

Slow-Release Version 4

$10 M   8   6   4   2   0

Reward (NPV)

Legume N-2

Vigor-B

Oysters

White Elephants

Adapted from SDG Method

Circle Size = resources (annual) per project

Exhibit 7.10B: Alternate Version of Agro's Risk-Return Bubble Diagram
(2 buckets)

Pearls

Bread and Butter

Probability Success (Scored) — High / Low

B A C

Spread-Ease

Soya-44

Charcoal-Base

D

Encapsulated

Slow-Release Version 4

$10 M   8   6   4   2   0

Reward (Scored)

Legume N-2

Vigor-B

Oysters

White Elephants

Reward = .3Str + .3MA + .4RR
Probability = .4PA + .25Syn + .35Pts
Factors are from scoring model – Exhibit 7.5

Adapted from Specialty Minerals

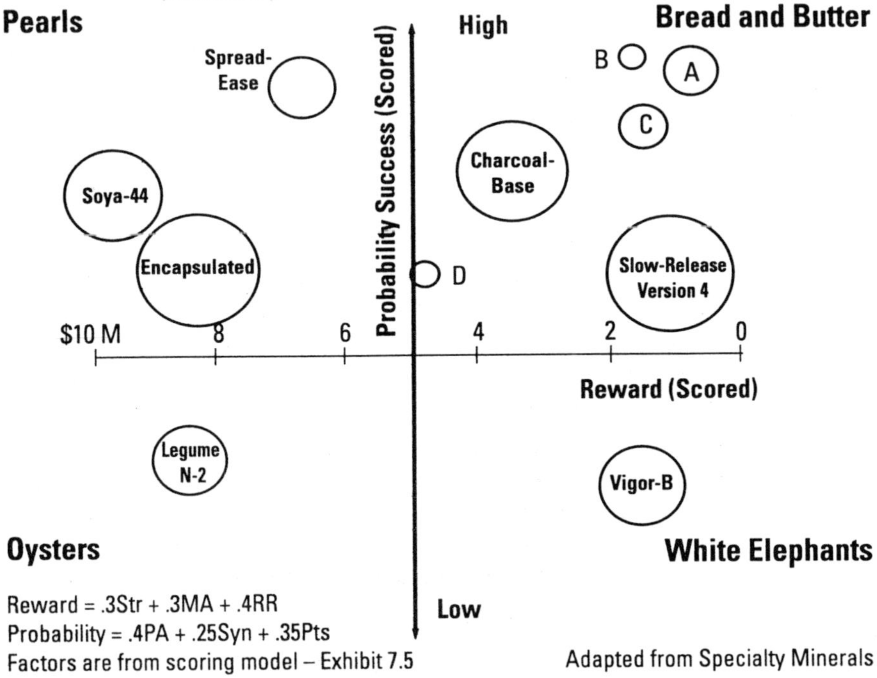

Exhibit 7.11: Agro's Ellipse Bubble Diagram

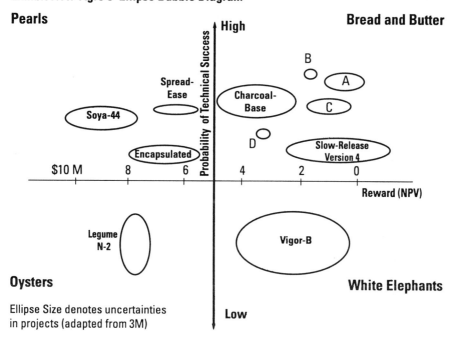

Ellipse Size denotes uncertainties
in projects (adapted from 3M)

Exhibit 7.12: Agro's Spending Breakdowns

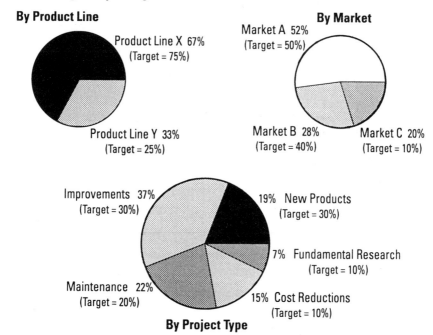

Numbers in parentheses denote desired spending splits (see Agro's Strategy Exhibit 6.4)

- Product Line split: Exhibit 7.12 reveals that projects for Product Line X accounted for about 67% of spending (versus a desired 75%). This 8% gap was relatively small as a percent, so no corrective actions were taken.
- Market split: Projects targeted at Market B accounted for 28% of the spend; this is far short of the goal of 40%. Further, projects for Market C accounted for far more than the goal (20% versus a target of 10%). Corrections were agreed to here via a Portfolio Balance Factor. Market B's PBF was set at 1.1 to encourage more projects here, while Market C's PBF was set at 0.9. Recall from Exhibit 7.9 the application of these PBFs in the calculation of Agro's adjusted Total Project Scores, which then were used to prioritize projects.
- Project Type: Strategic buckets were established a priori for the six project types. Only two types are considered in Exhibits 7.10A to 7.12. They are new products and product improvements (goal: 30% spending on each, or a 50-50 split). As shown in Exhibit 7.12, the desired spending levels were not achieved. Too much was going to product improvements and not enough to genuine new products. Sadly for Agro, it was simply a matter of not enough really good new product concepts in the pipe, and far too many product improvements proposed. Management decided to remain with these desired splits, and took action to stimulate the conception of more high quality new product projects for the next year.

Corrections and Adjustments

The Portfolio Review and discussion results in corrections to the mix of projects (i.e., corrects gate decisions already made) and in adjustments to the gating model itself (i.e., creates a shift in the mix of projects for the up-coming time period):

- Kill decisions: Some projects might be killed outright (e.g., those with low scores; or voted not strategically important). In effect, the portfolio meeting overrides (or takes the place of) a gate meeting. The hope is that Kill decisions here are rare. They should have been made at gate meetings!
- Immediate Go decisions: Some projects are designated as Strategic Imperatives and elevated to Go's or Top Priority (maximum spend).
- Adjustments to the gating scheme: A final result of the Portfolio Review is consensus on the need to adjust the balance of projects during the next period to better reflect both the desired balance and strategic priorities. For example, the decision might be that there are too many projects aimed at Market C and not enough at Market B. Next steps would aim to correct this imbalance over the next time period via the use of a Portfolio Balance Factor for gates; that is, the PBFs for different types of projects are decided here.

Example: Agro's adjustment and correction decisions:

▶ There were no strategic imperatives.

▶ Nor were any projects on the Hold list moved to active projects.

▶ A decision was made to seek resources for the two top-rated Hold projects, *N-2 Fix* and *Slow-Release*.

▶ *Vigor-B* was identified as problematic (a White Elephant) and killed off via a subsequent gate meeting.

▶ It was agreed that Market B projects were under-represented in the portfolio, and that Market C projects over-represented. Hence, the PBF was set at 1.1 for Market B and 0.9 for Market C to provide needed adjustments to gate decisions.

Portfolio Balance Factors

Recall that Portfolio Balance Factors can be agreed to for several project dimensions:

Market Type: Note the example above with PBFs for Market B projects versus Market C.

Product Type: This is similar, but for product lines – in order to tilt the scales for or against more projects in given product lines, balance factors are used.

Project Types: The conclusion at the portfolio meeting might be that there are too many minor projects – tweaks and modifications – and not enough major or genuine product developments. Portfolio Balance Factors can be agreed to, such that the scoring model used at gates would start to favor the major projects.

Risk and Reward: The bubble diagram may reveal too many small reward projects; or perhaps not enough high risk projects. Portfolio Balance Factors, again, can be constructed to tilt the scales at the gates.

Project Newness: The conclusion might be that there are too many projects towards the lower left of the newness matrix (Exhibit 4.2 in Chapter 4), and that we need more product and business development projects, and fewer share maintenance projects.

The point to note is that the Portfolio Review scans the list of projects, ensures that the ranking and prioritization is correct and, then, adjusts for balance. Corrections are made to the list of active and on-hold projects. Adjustments are also made via the Portfolio Balance Factors to be used at gate meetings throughout the successive year.

In Conclusion: An Integrated Decision System

The Portfolio Management Process ideally is an integrated decision system (see the full model in Exhibit 7.13).

At the top centre is the Strategy for the BU. This is the driver, because strategy starts when you start spending money. So the *choice of new product projects is the operationalization of strategy*. Recall that Strategy in our context includes the BU's business and its new product strategy. The latter specifies the new product goals for the BU, the arenas of focus (e.g., markets, product types and technologies), and ideally the desired spending splits across these, or in terms of project types.

Next, there is the new product process or Stage-Gate model, to the right in Exhibit 7.13. Its focus is on individual projects: the "fingers". The gates in the new product process must be working well in order that the total Portfolio Management Process performs. Note that the gates are where most of the on-going Go/Kill decisions are made on projects, and where resources are allocated. Gates can be constructed around a set of Must Meet or culling (knock-out) criteria, and also a set of Should Meet

Exhibit 7.13: The Total Portfolio Management Process (PMP) Linking Strategy, the Portfolio Review and the NP Process or Stage-Gate Model

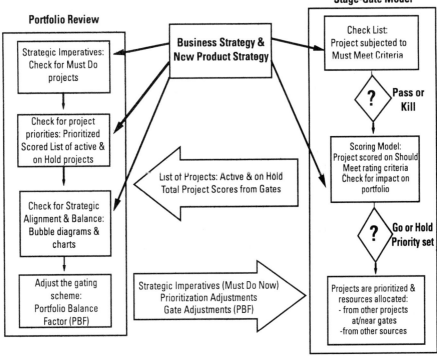

The Portfolio Review feeds the Stage-Gate Model; and the Stage-Gate Model feeds the Portfolio Review. Both Models are in sync and driven by Strategy.

items, which are scored and added via a scoring model. Criteria here include items which capture strategic fit and importance, value of the project to the BU, and likelihood of success. The Total Project Score becomes the key input to the Go/Kill decision at the gate, and also a key ranking criterion for use in prioritizing projects.

Then there is the Portfolio Review (left side in Exhibit 7.13). If the gates consider the "fingers", then the Portfolio Review looks at the "fist". It is holistic in nature and enables management to stand back to consider all projects – those which are active versus those on hold – together. Strategic imperatives may be identified: "must do now" projects. The Prioritized Scored List derived from gate decisions and the gate scoring model enable projects to be ranked against each other. Decisions may be made to deprioritize some and to elevate others. The balance of the portfolio is also reviewed using various bubble diagrams and pie charts. The risk-reward breakdown and spending breakdowns by market, product type and newness are topics of discussions here. Again, decisions may be made to re-prioritize certain projects. Finally, adjustments are made to the gating process via choice of Portfolio Balance Factors – correction factors to be applied at the gates to tilt the scales in favor of certain desired types of projects.

If all three elements of the process exist – Strategy, the Stage-Gate Process, and the Portfolio Review (with its various models and tools) – then a harmonized system should yield excellent portfolio choices: projects that deliver economic pay-offs, mirror the business's strategy, and achieve the BU's goals for new products. But if any piece of the PMP in Exhibit 7.13 is not working – for example, if there is no clearly defined strategy, or if the new product gating process is broken – the results are less than satisfactory.

****

New products are the leading edge of your business strategy. The product choices you make today determine what your business's product offerings and market position will be in five years. Making the right choices today is critical. Portfolio management and new product project selection is fundamental to business success. Make sure that you have the tools you need to make these right choices – an effective Portfolio Management Process – in your business!

References and Notes

Chapter 1

1. Archer, N.P. and Ghasemzadeh, F., "Project Portfolio Selection Techniques: A Review and a Suggested Integrated Approach", Innovation Research Centre Working Paper No. 46, McMaster University, 1996.

2. Baker, N.R., "R&D project selection models: an assessment", *IEEE Transactions on Engineering Management*, Vol. EM-21, No. 4:165-170, 1974.

3. Baker, N.R. and Pound, W.H., "R&D project selection: Where we stand", *IEEE Transactions on Engineering Management*, EM-11, No. 4:124-134, 1964.

4. Bard, J.F., Balachandra, R. and Kaufmann, P.E., "An interactive approach to R&D project selection and termination", *IEEE Transactions on Engineering Management*, 35(3):139-146, 1988.

5. Belton, V., "Project planning and prioritization in the social services - an OR contribution", *Journal of the Operational Research Society*, 44(2):115-124, 1993.

6. Cooley, S.C., Hehmeyer, J. and Sweeney, P.J., "Modelling R&D resource allocation", *Research Management*, 29(1):40-49, 1986.

7. Cooper, R.G., *Winning at New Products*, 2nd edition, Addison Wesley, Reading, Mass., 1993.

8. Cooper, R.G., "Third-generation new product processes", *Journal of Product Innovation Management*, 11:3-14, 1994.

9. Cooper, R.G. and Kleinschmidt, E.J. "Benchmarking firm's new product performance & practices", Engineering Management Review, 23(3):112-120, 1995.

10. Cooper, R.G. and Kleinschmidt, E.J., "Winning businesses in product development: Critical success factors", Research Technology Management, 39(4):18-29, 1996.

11. Czinkota, M. and Kotabe, M., "Product development the Japanese way", *The Journal of Business Strategy*, November/December: 31-36, 1990.

12. Danila, N., "Strategic evaluation and selection of R&D projects", *R&D Management*, 19(1):47-62, 1989.

13. De Maio, A, Verganti, R. and Corso, M., "A multi-project management framework for new product development", *European Journal of Operational Research*, 78(2):178-191, 1994.

14. Erickson, T. J., "Worldwide R&D management: concepts and applications", *Columbia Journal of World Business*, 25(4):8-13, 1990.

15. Griffin, A. and Page, A.L., "An interim report on measuring product development success and failure," *Journal of Product Innovation Management*, 9(1):291-308, 1993.

16. Hall, D.L. and Naudia, A. "An interactive approach for selecting IR&D projects", *IEEE Transactions on Engineering Management*, 37(2):126-133, 1990.

17. Jackson, B., "Decision methods for selecting a portfolio of R&D projects", *Research Management*, September-October: 21-26, 1983.

18. Khorramshahgol, R. and Gousty, Y., "Delphic goal programming (DGP): a multi-objective cost/benefit approach to R&D portfolio analysis", *IEEE Transactions on Engineering Management*, EM-33(3):172-175, 1986.

19. Liberatore, M.J., "An extension of the analytic hierarchy process for industrial R&D project selection and resource allocation", *IEEE Transactions on Engineering Management*, EM-34(1):12-18, 1987.

20. Liberatore, M. J., "A decision support system linking research and development project selection with business strategy", *Project Management Journal*, 19(5):14-21, 1988.

21. Lilien, G.L. and Kotler, P., *Marketing Decision Making: A Model-Building Approach*, Harper & Row Publishers: New York, 1983.

22. Parts of this are taken from Matheson, J.E., Menke, M.M. and Derby, S.L., "Improving the quality of R&D decision: a synopsis of the SDG approach," *Journal of Science Policy and Research Management* (in Japanese), 4(4), 1989. See also reference No. 2 for Chapter 3.

23. Morris, P.A., Teisberg, E.O. and Kolbe, A.L., "When choosing R&D projects, go with the long shots", *Research Technology Management*, 34:35-49, 1991.

24. Page, Albert L., "Assessing New Product Development Practices and Performance: Establishing Crucial Norms", *Journal of Product Innovation Management*, 10(4): 273-290, 1993.

25. Adapted from *Third Generation R&D, Managing the Link to Corporate Strategy,* by Roussel, P., Saad, K. and Erickson, T., Harvard Business School Press & Arthur D. Little Inc, Boston:Mass.,1991.

26. Schmidt, R. L., "A model for R&D project selection with combined benefit, outcome and resource interactions", *IEEE Transactions on Engineering Management*, 40(4):403-410, 1993.

27. Souder, W.E. and Mandakovic, T., "R&D project selection models", *Research Management*, 29(4):36-42, 1986.

28. Taggart, J H. and Blaxter, T.J., "Strategy in pharmaceutical R&D: a portfolio risk matrix", *R & D Management*, 22(3):241-254, 1992.

29. Weber, R., Werners, B. and Zimmermann, H.J., "Planning models for research and development", *European Journal of Operational Research*, 48(2):175-188, 1990.

30. Wheelwright, S. C. and Clark, K. B., "Creating project plans to focus product development", *Harvard Business Review*, 70(2):70-82, 1992.

31. Wind, Y. and Mahajan, V., "New product development process: a perspective for reexamination", *Journal of Product Innovation Management*, 5(4).304-310, 1988.

32. Yorke, D. A. and Droussiotis, G., "The use of customer portfolio theory: an empirical survey", *Journal of Business & Industrial Marketing*, 9(3):6-18, 1994.

33. Zahedi, Fatemeh, "The Analytic Hierarchy Process - A Survey of the Method and its Applications", *Interfaces*, 16(4):96-108, 1986.

Chapter 2

1. Cooper, R.G., *Winning at New Products*, 2nd edition, Addison Wesley, Reading, Mass., 1993.

2. Cooper, R.G. "Third-generation new product processes", *Journal of Product Innovation Management,* 11:3-14, 1994.

3. See reference Chapter 3, no. 2.

Chapter 3

1. Roussel, Philip, Saad, Kamal and Erickson, Tamara, *Third Generation R&D, Managing the Link to Corporate Strategy*, Harvard Business School Press & Arthur D. Little Inc., Boston: Massachusetts, 1991.

2. Taken from the Strategic Decisions Group (SDG). For more information refer to David Matheson, James E. Matheson and Michael M. Menke, "Making Excellent R&D Decisions", *Research Technology Management*, November-December 1994, pp. 21-24 and Patricia Evans, "Streamlining Formal Portfolio Management", *Scrip Magazine*, February, 1996.

3. Taken from internal 3M documents: Dr. Gary L. Tritle, "New Product Investment Portfolio"

4. Source: discussions with Tom Chorman, Corporate New Ventures Group, Procter & Gamble.

Chapter 4

1. Adapted from E. Roberts and C. Berry, "Entering new businesses: selecting strategies for success", *Sloan Management Review*, Spring, 1983, pp. 3-17.

2. For more information refer to Bob Gill, Beebe Nelson and Steve Spring, "Seven Steps to Strategic New Product Development", in *The PDMA Handbook of New Product Development* edited by Milton Rosenau, Jr., Abbie Griffin, George Castellion and Ned Anchuetz, John Wiley & Sons, Inc.: New York, 1996, pp. 19-34.

Chapter 5

1. Source: Exxon Chemical, Product Innovation Process (company brochure).

Chapter 6

1. For more information on the Boston Consulting Group's Growth-Share Matrix refer to B. Heldey, "Strategy and the Business Portfolio", *Long Range Planning*, 1977; for more information on the General Electric Approach refer to George Day, *Analysis for Strategic Marketing Decisions*, 1986, West Publishing, St. Paul, MN. and La Rue Hosner, *Strategic Management*, Prentice-Hall, Englewood Cliffs.

2. See Robert G. Cooper and Elko J. Kleinschmidt"Benchmarking Firm's New Product Performance & Practices", *Engineering Management Review*, Vol. 23, No. 3, 1995.

Chapter 7

1. For more information on Stage-Gate and the new product process see: Cooper, R.G., *Winning at New Products*, 2nd edition, Addison Wesley, Reading, Mass., 1993.

2. For more information on ProBE and how it can help your organization benchmark the new product development process, contact the authors.